ADHD PARENT COMPLEX CHILD:

Guiding Your Child with Love - A Journey to Become a Yell-Free and Frustration-Free Parent [III EDITION]

Copyright © 2023

Jennifer Mindlin

TABLE OF CONTENTS

1 INTRODUCTION

Attention Deficit Hyperactivity Disorder, or ADHD, is a term many people have heard but often misunderstand. It's a complex neurological condition that impacts many facets of life, affecting children and adults. If you're reading this, you may be seeking understanding, support, and strategies to navigate life with an ADHD-affected child.

Understanding ADHD

ADHD affects the brain's ability to concentrate and pay attention, leading to impulsivity, hyperactivity, and inattention. But understanding what this means in everyday terms can be tricky. Is every fidgety child ADHD-affected? Can children with ADHD ever focus? Will they grow out of it? Many parents ask these questions, and the answers aren't always straightforward.

Recognizing ADHD

Distinguishing normal childhood behavior from ADHD is not simple. Most children forget homework, daydream, or act irrationally at times. What sets ADHD apart is the frequency and intensity of these behaviors, making day-to-day living overwhelming and frustrating for both the child and the caregivers. The task ahead for parents, teachers, and caregivers is to recognize these signs and learn effective strategies to manage them. It's not just about identifying a problem; it's about understanding the underlying condition and embracing solutions.

Debunking Myths

Many misconceptions about ADHD need to be clarified:

- **Myth:** Every child with ADHD is hyperactive.
  - o **Fact:** Not all children with ADHD exhibit hyperactivity symptoms; attention issues might be the primary concern.
- **Myth:** Kids with ADHD will find it hard to pay attention to anything.
  - o **Fact:** ADHD-affected children can concentrate on various activities, but focusing on repetitive or boring tasks is challenging.
- **Myth:** Kids with ADHD can decide to behave better.
  - o **Fact:** Despite their best efforts, ADHD-affected children may struggle with quietness or attentiveness. It's not willful disobedience.
- Myth: Kids will eventually outgrow ADHD.
  - o Fact: Most cases persist into adulthood, making early intervention crucial.
- **Myth:** Medication is the only effective treatment for ADHD.

o **Fact:** Along with medication, many treatments include behavior therapy, nutrition, exercise, and support in various environments.

Moving Forward

As we delve into this book, you'll discover a comprehensive guide to understanding, accepting, and managing ADHD. You'll find tools and techniques tailored to support your unique journey with your ADHD-affected child. Together, we'll explore ways to turn daily challenges into opportunities for growth and connection.

2 ADHD TREATMENT

2.1.1 How ADHD Affects Children

Children with ADHD may present a challenging puzzle for parents and teachers. The common symptoms include:

- **Easily Distracted:** They may struggle to focus on tasks, often forgetting instructions and losing interest quickly.
- **Hyperactive:** Common traits include constant fidgeting, inability to sit still, and careless mistakes.
- **Impulsive:** Irrational actions and emotional outbursts may occur without warning.

These behaviors might be dismissed as normal childhood phases, but the consistency and intensity set ADHD apart. Understanding and managing these behaviors can feel overwhelming, even leading to self-doubt among caregivers. Recognizing that children with ADHD may lack inherent self-regulating skills is essential for parents. Education about ADHD and learning effective strategies can significantly improve the child's quality of life.

2.1.2 Brief History of ADHD

The journey to understanding ADHD has been long and fascinating:

- 1798: Alexander Crichton recognized distractibility in individuals.
- 1902: Sir George Frederic noted cases of impulsivity and attention problems in children.
- 1932: Hyperkinetic disorder was identified, marking a connection to the inability to remain still.
- 1937: Charles Bradley discovered Benzedrine's effectiveness, leading to later medications like methylphenidate (Ritalin).

- 1968: ADHD was first listed in DSM-II as a hyperkinetic reaction, evolving into ADHD in 1987.

The history of ADHD is filled with significant milestones and reveals our growing comprehension of this complex condition.

2.1.3   Data and Statistics for ADHD

The prevalence and complexity of ADHD continue to intrigue researchers:
- Diagnosed Children: About 6 million American children have ADHD, a noticeable increase from 4.5 million in 2003 to 6.1 million in 2016.
- Age Distribution:
  - 2.4 million aged 6 to 11
  - 388,000 aged 2 to 5
  - 3.3 million aged 12 to 17
- Gender Difference: Males are at higher risk compared to females.
- Associated Conditions: ADHD often coexists with other issues like anxiety, conduct problems, autism spectrum disorder, Tourette syndrome, and depression.

These statistics underscore the importance of understanding ADHD and its impact on children's lives and families.

2.2 Causes of ADHD and Risk Factors

Understanding ADHD involves looking at genetic, environmental, and biological factors. The complexity of the disorder has led to continued research and evolving theories. Below are some of the established causes and risk factors:

Genes and ADHD
- Genetic Influence: ADHD often runs in families, indicating a strong genetic component.
- Specific Genes: Particularly, genes linked to dopamine receptors, like the DRD4 gene, have been associated with ADHD.
- Multiple Genes: It's believed that more than one gene may be involved, making the genetic contribution complex.

Neurotoxins and ADHD
- Lead: Exposure to lead in children is associated with hyperactivity, impulsivity, and inattention.
- Pesticides: Organophosphate pesticides used on lawns and agricultural products have also been linked to ADHD.

Nutrition and ADHD

Food Dyes and Preservatives: Some believe these might influence ADHD, particularly hyperactivity, but conclusive evidence is lacking.

What Doesn't Cause ADHD

Myths: Common misconceptions include blaming video games, TV watching, excess sugar, poor parenting, and poverty.

Exacerbating Factors: Though not caused, these factors may worsen ADHD symptoms.

2.3 Signs and Symptoms of ADHD

ADHD is a complex disorder with diverse symptoms that can often be mistaken for typical developmental behaviors. These symptoms can be categorized into:

1. Hyperactive, Impulsive, and Inattentive Behavior: The most common form of ADHD.
2. Predominantly Inattentive: Often overlooked but significant in its impact on school performance and social interactions.
3. Predominantly Impulsive and Hyperactive: More easily noticeable due to disruptive behaviors.

Early recognition and intervention are essential for helping children with ADHD adapt and succeed.

2.3.1 Identifying ADHD at Different Ages

ADHD's persistent and disruptive characteristics, compared to typical developmental behavior, can become more apparent as children grow older, especially during school.

2.3.1.1 Inattentiveness in ADHD

Inattentiveness in ADHD can present in different forms:

- **Difficulty Listening:** Appears to be daydreaming or lost in thought.
- **Frequently Misplacing Items:** Trouble keeping track of belongings.
- **Easily Distracted and Bored with Tasks:** Losing focus on non-engaging activities.
- **Incomplete Tasks:** Struggling to finish tasks due to lack of focus.
- **Difficulty Following Instructions:** Trouble understanding and recalling directions.
- **Careless Mistakes:** Overlooking details or making errors due to lack of concentration.

These symptoms might be more subtle but can significantly impact a child's academic and social functioning. Addressing these challenges through behavioral therapy, educational accommodations, or medication can equip children with ADHD to succeed in various aspects of their lives.

2.3.1.2 Hyperactivity in ADHD

Hyperactivity remains the most obvious sign of ADHD, usually exhibited in most children. Some will remain quiet and still, but children with ADHD are always on the move. You'll see them trying to do many things simultaneously, and they usually quickly move from one activity to another. It is also difficult to get them to remain in one position. They will shake their legs, tap their feet, or drum with their fingers.

Symptoms of Hyperactivity in Children

Hyperactivity is a distinct and often noticeable sign of ADHD. It's characterized by constant motion, restlessness, and difficulty staying still. This aspect can manifest in various ways:

- **Quick Temper:** Prone to frustration and emotional outbursts.
- **Excessive Talking:** They may interrupt others and have difficulty waiting for their turn in conversations.
- **Restlessness:** Constant movement, including climbing, running, or fidgeting, even when inappropriate.
- **Inability to Relax:** Struggles with engaging in calm activities, preferring high-energy ones.
- **Constant Fidgeting:** Engaging in repetitive movements, possibly as a coping mechanism for focus or excess energy.

2.3.1.3 Impulsivity in ADHD

Impulsivity in ADHD relates to challenges with self-control and may cause children to seem disrespectful or peculiar, though this isn't necessarily true. Symptoms include:

- **Uncontrolled Emotions:** Disproportionate emotional outbursts, tantrums, and difficulty maintaining relationships.
- **Interrupting and Inappropriate Speech:** Struggles with social cues, resulting in interruptions or inappropriate comments.
- **Irrational Actions without Consideration:** Makes hasty decisions without regard for consequences.

- **Quick Guessing Instead of Problem-Solving:** Prefers rapid guesses over thoughtful problem solving, affecting academic performance.
- **Intrusion into Personal Space:** Struggles with recognizing and respecting boundaries, leading to uncomfortable situations.

2.3.2 Symptoms at Different Ages

Understanding the different manifestations of ADHD at various life stages can help in early identification, diagnosis, and appropriate intervention.

Symptoms of ADHD in Preschool-grade 2 Kids

- Fidgeting, getting up, or talking unnecessarily, even during quiet activities, makes it difficult for them to concentrate.
- Struggling to follow directions, which can lead to misunderstandings and incomplete tasks
- Difficulty remembering things, even recently taught concepts like simple arithmetic, resulting in frustration.
- Inability to do tasks slowly or patiently, often causing accidents or unfinished work
- Becoming angry or upset easily, even over minor issues, making it hard to handle conflict or disappointment
- Taking things without permission, resulting in trust issues and disciplinary actions

Symptoms of ADHD in Grades 3-7 Kids

- Struggling to follow multi-step directions, making it challenging to complete more complex tasks
- Acting or saying things impulsively, often leading to social misunderstandings
- Rushing through homework and making careless mistakes affecting academic performance
- Taking longer to complete assignments, even simple ones, leads to feelings of inadequacy.
- Clowning around and seeking attention from classmates results in distractions and strained relationships
- Restlessness during school assemblies or field trips, especially if they are not engaging, causes disruptions.

Symptoms of ADHD in Teens and Adults

- Difficulty making and maintaining friendships due to inconsistent behavior and communication
- Struggling to keep track of deadlines and recording assignments, leading to poor time management and organization
- Not considering the consequences of their actions, resulting in risky or irresponsible behavior.
- Disinterest in tasks perceived as boring, affecting motivation and perseverance
- Spacing out while reading or during other similar activities makes it difficult to absorb information.
- Needing to read information multiple times or asking others to repeat what they've said affecting efficiency and comprehension

The symptoms of ADHD can be associated with emotional, academic, and social difficulties. Specific criteria must be met before a diagnosis can be established. ADHD may be linked to significant behavioral issues, neurological conditions, and learning or developmental disabilities. Consultation with a professional to assess symptoms and receive an accurate diagnosis is essential.

2.3.3   What Makes ADHD Symptoms Worse?

- Certain factors might exacerbate the appearance of ADHD symptoms, although this doesn't mean that ADHD is necessarily worsening. Such factors include:
- **Performing Tasks Without Support:** Increasing academic challenges without proper support can create struggles for a child with ADHD.
- **Misunderstanding and Punishment:** Misinterpreting behaviors may lead to undue criticism or punishment, affecting the child's self-esteem and social interactions.
- **Co-morbid Disorders:** ADHD may coexist with other psychiatric disorders like anxiety and depression, complicating the clinical picture.
- **Stress:** Various life stressors can exacerbate ADHD symptoms, making management more complex.

2.4 Types of ADHD

ADHD is a complex and multifaceted disorder with various presentations that can manifest differently throughout an individual's life. Understanding these types allows for better recognition and treatment. The DSM-5 provides three main classifications for ADHD:

- Predominantly Inattentive Type: Characterized mainly by difficulties with attention.
- Predominantly Hyperactive-Impulsive Type: Mainly involves hyperactivity and impulsivity.
- Combined Type (Mixed): Includes symptoms of both inattention and hyperactivity-impulsivity.

The recognition of these types is crucial, as symptoms can shift with age, often transitioning from hyperactivity in childhood to predominance of inattention in later years. The understanding that ADHD is not a deliberate behavior but a neurological condition is essential for parents, educators, and others involved in caring for someone with ADHD.

2.4.1 Inattentive Type ADHD

The inattentive presentation of ADHD represents those who primarily struggle with attention deficits without hyperactivity. Here's a summary of the symptoms and characteristics:

- Forgetfulness: Regularly forgetting daily activities, chores, or appointments.
- Lack of Attention to Detail: Frequently making careless mistakes, affecting performance in school or work.
- Distractibility: Easily distracted by internal thoughts or external stimuli, hindering focus.
- Difficulty in Sustaining Attention: Struggling to pay attention to tasks, even recreational ones.
- Frequent Loss of Items: Often losing belongings, causing disorganization.
- Selective Hearing: Appearing not to listen, leading to communication problems.
- Avoidance of Mental Effort: Disliking or avoiding mentally demanding tasks.
- Organizational Struggles: Difficulty in managing belongings, time, or responsibilities.

- Failure to Complete Instructions: Often not finishing tasks, causing conflict with others.
- Poor Time Management: Struggling with punctuality and estimating the time required for tasks.
- Daydreaming: Regular disengagement and daydreaming affect social interactions.

These symptoms can overlap with typical child behaviors, so distinguishing between what is a normal phase and what might indicate ADHD is vital. Professional evaluation is essential if these behaviors consistently affect the child's daily life, relationships, and academic performance.

2.4.2   Hyperactivity and Impulsivity Type ADHD

The hyperactivity and impulsivity type of ADHD represents individuals who primarily show significant hyperactivity and impulsiveness. Here's an overview of the symptoms and features:
- Interrupting Others: Constantly interrupting games or conversations, leading to difficulties in social interaction.
- Inability to Sit Still: Frequent fidgeting, tapping, or squirming, which can be disruptive in various settings.
- Lack of Patience: Struggling with waiting their turn, causing conflicts.
- Frequent Movement: Often, leaving their seat or moving around inappropriately.
- Excessive Talking: Talking non-stop, making listening and comprehension difficult.
- Inappropriate Climbing or Running: Engaging in risky behaviors may pose safety concerns.
- Constant Activity: Always on the go, driven by an inner motor.
- Struggles with Quiet Play: Difficulty engaging in quiet activities without causing disturbances.
- Impulsive Answers: Blurting out responses impulsively.

The hyperactivity-impulsivity type of ADHD shares some commonalities with the inattentive type and can co-occur with other developmental disabilities like autism.

2.4.3   Combined Type ADHD

The combined type of ADHD represents individuals who exhibit characteristics of both hyperactivity-impulsivity and inattentive types. Here's an insight into this type:
- Dual Presentation: The presence of both inattentive and hyperactive-impulsive symptoms.

- Most Common Form: Identified by the National Institutes of Health as the prevalent type of ADHD in children.
- Predominance of Hyperactivity: Especially among preschool-age children.

Diagnosing ADHD requires a holistic assessment involving mental health professionals. This evaluation ensures that other developmental disabilities or learning disorders are not mistakenly identified as ADHD or overlooked.

Through proper diagnosis, therapeutic interventions, educational accommodations, and family support, individuals with ADHD can navigate the challenges of the condition. The ultimate goal is to help them harness their unique abilities and strengths, supporting their growth into productive and fulfilling lives.

2.5 A breakdown of ADHD behavior compared to normal behavior

Understanding the difference between ADHD and normal, age-appropriate behavior is crucial for recognizing the signs of ADHD and distinguishing them from temporary behavioral issues. The following examples illustrate these differences across various age groups:

Roy's Story (Child Example):

- ADHD Behavior: Roy's inability to grasp instructions, struggles with organization, consistent distraction, and lack of interest in activities illustrate symptoms typical of ADHD. These behaviors persist and are chronic, reflecting an underlying neurodevelopmental disorder.
- Normal Behavior: In contrast, a typical child might exhibit some of these behaviors due to temporary factors such as anger, stress, or family problems, but they usually subside within six months. A normal child, Roy's age may lose interest in a task if it's not engaging but can generally concentrate and follow instructions when motivated.

Mr. Walter's Story (Adult Example):

- ADHD Behavior: Mr. Walter's over-analysis of a simple greeting with Mr. Jesse, persistent worrying about a minor event, and resultant delay in his work project illustrate the intrusive thoughts and difficulty in focusing that can accompany ADHD in adults. His inability to move on from the incident and the effect on his sleep indicates how ADHD can permeate multiple aspects of life.
- Normal Behavior: A typical person might notice and interpret Mr. Jesse's busyness but would likely move on without overthinking the interaction. While anyone loses focus if a task is uninteresting, people without ADHD generally can direct and sustain their attention when necessary.

Mr. Richard's Story (Adult Example):

- ADHD Behavior: His easy infuriation by noise, heightened anxiety on the road, excessive sweating, and near accident are signs of hyperactivity and impulsiveness often linked to ADHD. These reactions aren't just occasional responses to stimuli but persistently affect his daily routines.
- Normal Behavior: While a normal individual might react to an obnoxious sound or feel stressed in traffic, these reactions typically wouldn't escalate to the extreme levels seen in Mr. Richard or persistently impact daily life.

Mr. Robins' Story (Young Adult Example):

- ADHD Behavior: As a freshman in college, Mr. Robins struggles with impulsive behaviors like interrupting in class, fidgeting, and lack of focus. These are not occasional slips but consistent patterns that likely hinder his academic and social life.
- Normal Behavior: Many college students might exhibit some of these behaviors, especially when adjusting to a new environment, but they wouldn't typically persist or interfere significantly with daily functioning.

Key Differences:

1. **Duration and Consistency:** ADHD-related behaviors persist and are consistent over time, often extending into adulthood. In contrast, normal behavior reflecting inattention is usually temporary and situation-dependent.
2. **Impact on Daily Functioning:** While everyone experiences moments of inattention, those with ADHD may find these symptoms significantly interfering with daily functioning, including social interactions, academic or work performance, and emotional well-being.
3. **Response to External Stimuli:** Individuals with ADHD may overreact or overthink simple events, leading to distraction and anxiety. A typical person might have momentary distractions but can usually process and move past them without lingering effects.
4. **Developmental Context:** ADHD symptoms can manifest differently across various life stages. While it may be harder to detect in children with supportive structures, the self-management demands of adulthood or college life may reveal the underlying disorder.
5. **Gender and Age:** It's important to recognize that ADHD can affect individuals of any gender and age. Misconceptions about ADHD primarily affecting young males can lead to underdiagnosis in others.

Conclusion:

The differences between ADHD-related behaviors and what might be considered normal are nuanced yet significant. Recognizing these differences is crucial for accurate diagnosis and appropriate support and treatment. ADHD goes beyond the occasional restlessness or impulsive action, and its chronic nature, severity, and impact on daily functioning set it apart. Early diagnosis, tailored interventions, and ongoing professional support can play a vital role in managing ADHD symptoms and promoting well-being for individuals of all ages.

2.6 ADHD Diagnosis and Differential Diagnosis

The diagnostic criteria for ADHD are detailed and specific. The diagnosis often involves multiple steps and collaboration among various professionals. Here's an overview of the typical diagnostic process:

- **Initial Screening:** Primary care providers may conduct an initial screening using standardized questionnaires or checklists completed by parents, teachers, and sometimes the individual.
- **Comprehensive Evaluation:** This includes a detailed medical history, physical examination, interviews with family members, and a review of school and work performance. The individual's behavior must meet specific criteria outlined in diagnostic guides such as the DSM-5 (Diagnostic and Statistical Manual of Mental Disorders, 5th Edition).
- **Behavioral Observations:** Healthcare providers may observe the individual's behavior in various settings or ask teachers and family members about their observations.
- **Exclusion of Other Conditions:** Other medical or psychological conditions that could explain the symptoms must be ruled out. These might include anxiety disorders, depression, learning disabilities, or other health issues.
- **Ongoing Monitoring:** ADHD is a chronic condition, and regular follow-up is needed to assess the effectiveness of treatment and make necessary adjustments.

Differential Diagnosis

Differential diagnosis is critical to the evaluation process, as other disorders or conditions may mimic ADHD symptoms. Some of these include:

- Anxiety Disorders: Symptoms such as restlessness, difficulty concentrating, and impulsivity can be seen in anxiety disorders, making them potentially confusable with ADHD.
- Depression: Lack of focus and difficulty with concentration may also be seen in depressive disorders.
- Learning Disabilities: Challenges in academic performance might not be due to ADHD but specific learning disabilities that require different interventions.
- Sleep Disorders: Lack of quality sleep can lead to symptoms similar to ADHD, such as inattention and hyperactivity.
- Substance Abuse: Substance abuse can lead to behaviors that might mimic ADHD.

Importance of Accurate Diagnosis

An accurate diagnosis of ADHD is not just about identifying the presence of the disorder but also understanding the individual's unique pattern of symptoms and functioning. This information is essential for developing an effective treatment plan, including medication, therapy, educational support, and lifestyle changes.

Conclusion

Diagnosing ADHD is a complex, multifaceted process that requires careful consideration of various factors and excluding other potential underlying conditions. It involves a combination of clinical assessments, behavioral observations, and collaboration with those who know the individual well, such as parents and teachers. The aim is to identify the disorder and tailor a treatment plan that meets the individual's unique needs. An accurate diagnosis can lead to effective management of ADHD, greatly enhancing the quality of life for the individual and their family. It underscores the importance of seeking professional evaluation and treatment from trained and experienced healthcare providers specializing in ADHD and related disorders.

2.7 Comorbidities

ADHD often exists with other psychological or neurological conditions known as comorbidities. This complex web can impact both the diagnosis and treatment of ADHD. This section aims to comprehensively understand these comorbidities and how they interact with ADHD.

- Tic Disorders: Including Tourette's Syndrome, characterized by involuntary, repetitive movements or sounds.
- Mood Disorders: Such as depression and bipolar disorder, often characterized by feelings of sadness or mood swings.
- Executive Function Challenges: Difficulty managing time, attention, planning, and organization.
- Learning Disabilities: Including dyslexia (reading), dysgraphia (writing), and dyscalculia (math).
- Motor Skill Difficulties: Problems with small (fine) and large (gross) motor skills and coordination.
- Language Disorders: Understanding or using spoken language can be problematic.
- Anxiety Disorders: Including generalized anxiety disorder and social anxiety disorder.
- Oppositional Defiant Disorder (ODD): Persistent angry or defiant behavior.

- Intermittent Explosive Disorder: Aggressive and violent outbursts.
- Substance Use Disorder: Issues with drugs or alcohol.
- Eating Disorders: Problems with eating patterns.
- Sleep Disorders: Including difficulty falling or staying asleep.
- Autism Spectrum Disorder: A developmental disorder affecting communication and interaction.

Impact on Treatment

Recognizing and addressing comorbidities is vital for crafting a well-rounded treatment plan. Often, a multifaceted approach that considers both ADHD and any comorbid conditions is required. Treatment might include medication, therapy, lifestyle changes, and specific interventions for the coexisting conditions.

2.8 Management of ADHD: Medication Options

- This chapter focuses on the medical management of ADHD (Attention Deficit Hyperactivity Disorder). Treatment options aim to alleviate symptoms and enhance the individual's daily life. While therapy, counseling, and education services can play a role, medications are often central to treatment. Note that medications manage symptoms but don't cure the disorder. Careful supervision and regular medical check-ups are vital to successful treatment.
- First-Line Treatment: Stimulant Medications
- Stimulant medications like methylphenidate and amphetamine derivatives are generally the first-line treatment for ADHD. These drugs have even been shown to reduce the risk of substance abuse in patients with ADHD. The primary stimulant drugs include:
- Methylphenidate
- Amphetamine derivatives (lisdexamfetamine and dexamphetamine)

2.8.1 Methylphenidate

Methylphenidate is a central nervous system stimulant commonly prescribed for ADHD.

Mechanism of Action

As a norepinephrine-dopamine reuptake inhibitor, it increases the activity of neurotransmitters Dopamine and Serotonin in the CNS, enhancing concentration, reducing fatigue, and increasing attention span.

Side Effects

Possible side effects range from loss of appetite, dizziness, and nausea, to serious problems like irregular heartbeat, mood changes, and blurred vision.

Usage Precautions

- Regularly check blood pressure, as it may elevate.
- Do not administer to children under six or those with hypersensitivity to the drug.
- Avoid in patients with glaucoma, severe hypertension, high thyroid levels, severe anxiety, or tension.
- Follow the prescribed dosage; if a dose is missed, do not double up with the next one.
- Gradual tapering under medical guidance is essential to avoid withdrawal symptoms like fatigue, depression, and sleep disturbances.

2.8.2   Lisdexamfetamine

Lisdexamfetamine, a central nervous system (CNS) stimulant, is another medication used in the treatment of ADHD, as well as binge eating disorders in adults. It's an amphetamine derivative, less commonly preferred than methylphenidate but has proven beneficial in managing ADHD symptoms.

Mechanism of Action

Lisdexamfetamine is a prodrug, which is converted into its active form, dextroamphetamine, in the body. This active form releases neurotransmitters from their storage sites and prevents their reuptake, increasing their concentration in the brain and thus stimulating the CNS. This action targets the primary symptoms of ADHD, such as inattention, hyperactivity, and impulsiveness.

Benefits

Aside from reducing the risk of substance abuse development, Lisdexamfetamine has enhanced overall well-being, academic benefits, and social gains.

Common Side Effects

The usual side effects of Lisdexamfetamine include but are not limited to:

Loss of appetite, Insomnia, Nausea, Weight loss, Anxiety, Diarrhea, Dry mouth, Irritability, Dizziness. Patients should seek medical attention immediately if experiencing any alarming symptoms such as allergic reactions, mental health issues, blurred vision, or heart problems.

Precautions

When utilizing Lisdexamfetamine for ADHD treatment, the following precautions must be considered:

- Heart and Stroke Risks: Caution must be exercised in patients with heart disease, high blood pressure, or other cardiovascular issues.
- MAOI Drugs Interaction: Combining with MAOI drugs can lead to a hypertensive crisis and must be avoided.

- Habit-forming Risk: Following the doctor's prescription is crucial since the drug can be habit-forming.
- Dosing Instructions: Typically taken in the morning, it can be consumed with or without food. Missed doses should be managed carefully, not doubling with the next one.

2.8.3   Dexamfetamine

Dexamfetamine, also known as Dextroamphetamine, is an Amphetamine derivative. As mentioned in the previous drug explanation, Lisdexamfetamine is a prodrug metabolized in the body to give L-lysine and Dextroamphetamine. Dextroamphetamine is the metabolite and the active substance of that prodrug. This drug has other health benefits apart from the treatment of ADHD. Dexamfetamine works by inhibiting the transportation of neurotransmitters in the CNS to their storage vesicle, thereby making them last longer in the brain to improve brain function and increase alertness. The ultimate goal of the medication is to improve the patient's quality of life. Generally, the drug is used to improve the ability to pay attention, improve focus, and improve behavioral patterns. Extra benefits include enhanced listening skills and the ability to organize tasks. Common side effects of the drug include headache, dry mouth, unpleasant taste, weight loss (especially in children), changes in sex drive, and constipation. Contact your doctor if you experience any of the following: excessive fatigue, mood changes, anxiety, aggressiveness, hallucinations, seizures, dizziness, blurred vision, slow speech, numbness, or growth retardation in children using this drug to treat ADHD.

Precautions

The drug should be used with caution in patients who are hypersensitive to any dextroamphetamine, lisdexamfetamine, or other component used in manufacturing, have a history of glaucoma, hypertension, high blood pressure, hyperthyroidism, bipolar disorder, depression, anxiety, are pregnant or breastfeeding, or are taking MAOI drugs. Tell your doctor about the other medications you are taking, as some can inhibit the action or decrease the absorption of the drug. Remember to consult your Physician or Pharmacist when taking the drug. Take the drug according to the prescription. The medication is given 1–3 times daily, with or without meals. Usually, the first dosage is taken in the morning. As stated earlier, a doctor will usually prescribe in low doses, which can be increased with continuous use. In this case, you can take the drug 4-6 hours apart.

2.8.4 Atomoxetine

Atomoxetine is a norepinephrine reuptake inhibitor normally taken orally and should be used by children at least 6 years old. One unique advantage of atomoxetine over other ADHD drugs is that it has little or no abuse potential. It can be used together with stimulant drugs to give a synergistic effect. On its own, the drug shows low response and treatment to ADHD, but it can inhibit the re-uptake of these neurotransmitters. Atomoxetine works by inhibiting the re-uptake of the brain's neurotransmitters and also prevents the storage of the neurotransmitters. Common side effects of atomoxetine include loss of appetite, weight loss, constipation, nausea, vomiting, fatigue, insomnia, irregular menses in women, and decreased libido and sexual activity. You should contact your doctor immediately if you experience difficulty urinating, irregular heartbeat, numbness, tingling sensation, or fainting. Rarely, the drug can cause liver issues, stroke, heart attack, decreased erection in men, and allergies like itching and rashes. Monitoring children closely for mood changes while on this drug is important.

Additionally, be sure to let your doctor know if you are hypersensitive to atomoxetine or any of its components, taking drugs in the MAOI class, have glaucoma, hyperthyroidism, high blood pressure, or stroke symptoms, or are on other medications that may interact with it. Atomoxetine can cause drowsiness and dizziness, so do not operate heavy machinery or drive while using the drug. When waking up, slowly stand up from the bed to prevent falling or fainting. Using the medicine may affect your ability to get a good night's sleep. Be sure to discuss any questions or concerns with your doctor or pharmacist. It is customary to take this medication in the morning, split into many doses. You may have it either as a snack or as a meal.

Precautions

Precautions for using Atomoxetine include closely monitoring children for mood changes, informing your doctor if you are hypersensitive to Atomoxetine or any of its components, taking caution when using it together with drugs in the MAOI class, informing your doctor if you have glaucoma, hyperthyroidism, high blood pressure, or stroke symptoms, being cautious about drug-drug interactions if you are on other medications, avoiding operating heavy machinery or driving because Atomoxetine can make you tired, and taking caution when standing up from the bed to avoid dizziness. Using Atomoxetine may affect your ability to get a good night's sleep. Be sure to discuss any questions or concerns with your doctor or pharmacist. It is customary to take this medication in the morning, split into many doses. You may have it either as a snack or as a meal.

2.8.5 Guanfacine

Guanfacine is a medication used in treating ADHD but is not typically a first-line drug of choice. It can also be used to manage high blood pressure. The drug's efficacy in treating ADHD is not as strong as the previously discussed drugs. This drug is an adrenergic receptor agonist, meaning it works by activating the adrenergic receptors in the central nervous system, which regulates blood pressure and neurotransmitter levels. It is also a serotonin agonist. Common side effects include dry mouth, dizziness, constipation, and fatigue. Contact your doctor immediately if you experience serious dizziness, irregular heartbeat, mood changes leading to suicidal thoughts, or allergic reactions such as itching or rashes. Precautions should be taken when using this drug, such as using it with caution if you are hypersensitive to guanfacine or any of the ingredients used in manufacturing, pregnant or breastfeeding, currently using other medications, or have a history of heart attack, stroke, or other medical conditions. It is important to note that the drug can cause drowsiness, so do not operate machinery or drive while using the medication. The medication can be taken orally once daily with or without food and at bedtime.

Precautions

It is important to take precautions when using guanfacine. If you are hypersensitive to guanfacine or any of the ingredients used in manufacturing, you should use the drug with caution. Pregnant or breastfeeding women should also be cautious when using guanfacine. Additionally, if you currently use other medications, check for drug-drug interactions before using guanfacine. If you have a history of heart attack, stroke, or other medical conditions, you should also be cautious when using guanfacine. It is worth noting that guanfacine can cause drowsiness, so you should not operate machinery or drive while using the medication. The drug should be taken orally once daily, with or without food, and at bedtime. If you experience severe side effects such as serious dizziness, irregular heartbeat, mood changes that may lead to suicidal thoughts, or allergic reactions like itching and rashes, seek medical attention immediately.

2.9 Advantages of ADHD

Attention Deficit Hyperactivity Disorder (ADHD) is most often characterized by inattention, hyperactivity, and impulsivity symptoms. However, it's vital to recognize that these traits can extend beyond mere challenges, giving rise to unique advantages for those affected by ADHD.

The common saying, "there is ability in disabilities," rings particularly true for individuals with ADHD. By embracing and managing these traits, many have learned to leverage them for success. Of course, it's essential to note that seeking a diagnosis and treatment for ADHD is still crucial. This understanding sets the stage for overcoming challenges and thriving despite this neurodevelopmental condition.

Hyperfocus and Creativity

One remarkable advantage of ADHD is the ability to hyperfocus, particularly when engaged in a passion. This trait has led to tremendous success for some individuals, like Mr. Wellington, an award-winning mural artist.

Wellington's academic struggles were offset by a passion for painting that was initially overlooked by his family. But under Dr. Caleb's guidance, Wellington's talents flourished. He found himself lost in the magic of painting and eventually turned his impulsivity into creativity. Wellington's hyperfocus helped him develop extraordinary skills and make a significant impact in the art world.

Such intense focus is not unique to those with ADHD but often manifests in an unparalleled ability to experiment, tweak, and innovate. People like Robin, who built airplane prototypes from folding cartons, exemplify this unique thinking approach. Despite his academic shortcomings, Robin's practical and outside-the-box thinking led to unexpected inventions and solutions, like fixing his father's car tires. Even Michael Phelps, one of the greatest Olympic swimmers, channeled his inner creativity to overcome the challenges posed by ADHD. His journey from struggling student to record-breaking athlete serves as an inspiration to many.

Humor and Divergent Thinking

Another fascinating aspect of ADHD is what researchers call "divergent thinking" or "flexible thinking." This unconventional way of processing information often leads to high humor and creativity.

Jasmine's story illustrates this point. Diagnosed with ADHD at 15, she was known for her impromptu classroom dance sessions and hilarious remarks. Her natural talent for comedy eventually found a place on the stand-up stage, where she turned confusion into entertainment. Jasmine's success in comedy and her advocacy for ADHD awareness demonstrates how unique thinking patterns can be transformed into a powerful strength.

In addition to humor, individuals with ADHD often surprise themselves, turning seemingly negative traits, like forgetfulness, into unexpected moments of joy. Mr. Edwin's habit of forgetting money in his pockets led to pleasant surprises, illustrating how ADHD traits can provide unexpected pleasure mechanisms.

Energy and Athletic Prowess

Energy is often seen as a disruptive trait in ADHD individuals, especially during childhood. However, this energy can become a powerful force for success when harnessed properly.

Lewis's story is a prime example. Initially perceived as problematic, his abundant energy was channeled into sprinting, leading to a gold medal at the Rio 2016 Olympics. Dr. Carlos's expert guidance helped transform what was once seen as a disability into an opportunity for greatness.

Conclusion

People with ADHD often possess traits that, when managed and nurtured, can lead to extraordinary achievements. From the ability to hyperfocus and think creatively to an abundance of energy and humor, these traits can be harnessed to create powerful change. While ADHD presents unique challenges, it also offers distinctive advantages. Through intentional practice, support, and self-awareness, these abilities can be unlocked and used as tools for success. Understanding and embracing the complexity of ADHD helps those affected by it thrive and expands our perspective on what it means to be uniquely human.

2 UNDERSTANDING YOUR CHILD'S CONDITION

2.1 Facts on Child Brain Development

Researchers are still learning about ADHD, as well as brain development. There are many indications that the differences in some components of the brain make it much harder for people with ADHD to concentrate and maintain focus, especially when they are not interested in it. ADHD is a neurodevelopmental disorder, which implies that some deficits can alter the normal development of a child's brain. However, this does not necessarily mean a negative impact on intelligence. The main effect of this deficit is an inability to regulate emotions and attention, resulting in hyperactivity and impulsivity. Some may also experience problems with organization.

2.1.1 Normal Brain Explained

For more than 20 years now, different studies have shown that about 95% of the total brain volume of a young adult is achieved at age 5 to 7. Also, research shows that the total cerebral volume (TCV) reaches its maximum before adolescence. A study involving 45 children aged 5 to 11, of which MRI scans were taken at two years intervals, revealed a noticeable brain expansion by 1 mm yearly. This expansion was mostly at the prefrontal cortex. Upon cross-sectional analysis, an age-related ventricular increase in the size of the TCV and a corresponding decrease in the lenticular nucleus and the thalamus were also seen. Studies have also identified that the cerebellum and the cerebrum are generally larger in boys than in girls. This is the main reason the cortical gray matter is also larger in boys than in girls. Other larger features in boys include the subcortical regions, the globus pallidus, and the putamen. The only feature that is larger in girls is caudate.

White and gray matter development

Longitudinal and cross-sectional brain analyses have shown a consistent increase in the volume of white matter within the pediatric age range. This increase was greater in the male gender, and a corresponding increase in myelination was observed within the same age range.

In a cross-sectional study performed using 110 adolescents and children between the ages of 4 to 17, the age-related changes in the neural tracts were examined. An increase in the white matter of the posterior portion and internal capsule of the left arcuate fasciculus was identified. White matter development was also seen in specific regions like the corpus callosum, where the increase was first identified, followed by a posterior growth during adolescence. The growth of gray matter follows a more heterogeneous pattern. In general, the gray matter decreases from childhood through to post-adolescence. However, the decrease does not follow a linear fashion. The general progression is a 13% increase and growth in the gray matter between ages 6 to 9, followed by a 5% decrease every decade.

2.1.2 ADHD Brain Explained

There are so many questions that surround ADHD. Some still ask if the condition is real or simply a lack of willpower, bad parenting, or lack of motivation. None of these are true, and such comments will only make you feel vulnerable, especially if you have a child with ADHD. One of the major things you should know is that there are several biological differences between the brain of a normal person and that of a person with ADHD. These differences can be divided into function, structure, and chemistry.

Brain Function

Until a few decades ago, there was a general lack of understanding of how the brain worked, but advancements in brain imaging today make it feasible to fully comprehend how the brain works. Use of the following techniques include:

- Functional magnetic resonance imaging (fMRI)

- Single-photon emission computer tomography (SPECT)
- Positron emission tomography (PET)

ADHD research showed that some brain regions had different blood flow levels in people with the disease compared to those who didn't. Additionally, reduced blood flow to the prefrontal areas has also been found. In general, a reduction in blood flow to the brain can ultimately decrease the brain's activity.

The brain's prefrontal region is the main house for different executive functions. It is the part responsible for tasks, including organizing, remembering, emotional reactions, paying attention, and planning. Research data suggests a relationship between ADHD and brain dysfunction. MRI suggests that people with ADHD usually have higher functional connectivity in some parts of the brain than others.

Brain Structure

Research has also revealed an obvious structural difference between a normal brain and an ADHD brain. People with ADHD usually have lesser brain volume, especially in five subcortical areas. This brings about an ultimate reduction in their brain size, and the difference is more in children than adults. In individuals with ADHD, the brain is never completely developed. In addition, the hippocampus and amygdala are smaller among those with ADHD, which is also intriguing. These two brain regions play an essential part in impulsiveness and emotional treatment.

Brain Chemistry

The brain is characterized by different communication networks, all implicated in transferring messages and information between brain cells (neurons). The gap between these neurons is known as a synapse. Before a message can be transported from one neuron to another, these synapses must be filled with chemical messengers called neurotransmitters. There are different types of neurotransmitters, and they all have different functions. In ADHD, noradrenaline and dopamine are the key neurotransmitters. The dopamine system is dis-regulated in an ADHD brain, unlike in a normal brain. An ADHD brain will either under-utilize dopamine or lack sufficient receptors or neurotransmitters.

2.1.3   Neuroimaging Patterns Predict ADHD Symptoms

Demographic and behavioral data, alongside MRI scans showing brain patterns, have helped in predicting some of the symptoms of ADHD in both children and adults. Evidence of this finding can be seen in the American Journal of Psychiatry, in which different researchers examined MRI scans of about 160 Australian children. These children were between 9 and 12 years of age. Four pervasive brain profiles were identified, indicative of certain ADHD symptoms. Advanced MRI modeling was used in documenting brain changes from different viewpoints. The aim was to identify common patterns through different anatomical scales that can be related to cognitive abilities or ADHD symptoms. The results obtained from this study suggest that some of the unique symptoms experienced by children with ADHD can be related to the biology of the brain. About 70 children in this study were diagnosed with ADHD, and up to 25 were receiving medications to help them manage the condition. During this study, different assessment strategies were employed, and the aim was to track demographic characteristics and symptoms. The assessments spanned over 4 hours, including a self-reported survey, parent questionnaire, and cognitive evaluation. Combining MRI scans, psychographic data, demographic data, and assessments allowed researchers to identify four different brain patterns. These patterns can be associated with demographic and behavioral profiles for application in predicting symptoms of ADHD in different groups of children.

1. **Development:** Children less developmentally mature have a higher tendency to become hyperactive. Such kids will need to receive medication for ADHD. Also, younger brain age is a common thing with ADHD children, especially those who are less developmentally mature.

2. **Cognitive Performance:** The identified patterns were also related to reduced cognitive performance, few hyperactivity symptoms, and higher irritability which is not associated with ADHD. Certain environment components were also identified. This includes maternal smoking, poor quality of life, and low parental education,

3. **Male Hyperactivity:** The profiles of children under this category suggest that male child has a higher tendency to become hyperactive, and this was further included from different rating scales of teachers and parents. Also, such kids are more likely to have comorbidity and other social problems. Pre-pubescent male children are more likely to experience these changes.

4. **Size of the Head:** While the academic achievements of boys and girls are related to their brain size, boys have a much greater brain capacity than girls. This is because academic performance, cognitive ability, and brain size are all interrelated.

Studies are ongoing, and the aim is to have a better and more advanced neurological understanding of ADHD.

2.1.4   Brain Maturation Delayed, Not Deviant, in ADHD Children

Children with ADHD have more difficulty with brain growth, especially with cortical development. They are prone to being distracted, which significantly impacts their attention and working memory, with the prefrontal lobe as the most impacted portion of the brain. There is currently a debate on whether delay in brain development is a cause of ADHD. Some think ADHD can be associated with a deviation from normal brain development. Different studies have been performed to help resolve this controversy. One such research was performed by Philip Shaw. This was a neuroanatomical study. The results of this research associated ADHD with a delay in brain maturation rather than a deviation in cortical maturation. In Shaw's research, the thickness of the cortex was measured in about 450 children, half of which were normal and the other half with ADHD. Brain scans from these children were taken twice over a three-year interval. Also, the participants in this research included young adults and preschoolers between 7 and 16 years. 92% of the children with ADHD had the combined type of ADHD. The cortical thickness was estimated from over 800 MRI scans, focusing on finding the age at which the cortical thickness peaked. Children without ADHD reached their peak cortical thickness at age 8. Those with ADHD didn't reach peak cortical thickness until age 10. The study also revealed that delay in cortical maturity was more evident in the lateral prefrontal cortex, a supportive feature for cognitive functions, such as executive attention control, suppressing inappropriate thoughts and responses, working memory, and evaluating reward contingencies. The primary motor cortex is the only area of the brain in which children with ADHD experience early maturation.

What is responsible for the delay?

According to Shaw and his team of researchers, genetic factors and psychostimulants had a major role. Psychostimulants are implicated because most of the participants in the study were on one psychostimulant or the other. The research team also suggested that the psychostimulants had trophic effects in the ADHD group. This is still possible even if the psychostimulants' impact on grey matter volume was not detected. Therefore, no one can argue that genetics is not a significant influence.

2.2 First Diagnosis

Inattentiveness, hyperactivity, and impulsivity are all characteristics of ADHD. CDC reports that 11% of U.S. youngsters have ADHD. This neurodevelopmental condition is diagnosed based on observed symptoms in children and adults. This chapter hopes to explore what should be done after the child's diagnosis has been reported.

Firstly, as a parent or a guardian of a child, it's normal to be emotional about what your ward is going through. However, you accept the diagnosis in the best interest of your child, yourself, and the community.

Acknowledgment of the diagnosis is important so that assistance can commence immediately. Knowing and accepting a challenge means problem-solving strategies can be employed or deployed. If you're in doubt about the diagnosis, consult another center with expertise in the diagnosis and management of ADHD as soon as possible so that the behavior of your child doesn't deteriorate.

Once you have accepted the diagnosis, you must know what ADHD is. This requires conscious or intentional study of relevant articles on ADHD. You have to understand the basics of ADHD, its symptoms, different medications pattern, differential diagnoses, psychotherapy, and all the relevant information that would be useful to your child's management and recovery. Another way to get information about ADHD is through a session with an ADHD, brain development, and children educator expert. They will explain how the brain works in normal and pathologic conditions like ADHD. Again, it's important that you have complete knowledge of ADHD; other people who relate to the child should also understand what ADHD means. This will help foster support for the child at home and in school. Examples of such persons are the teachers, friends, siblings, and relatives who constantly visit your home. Why must you divulge your ward's diagnosis to the teacher? Because the teacher acts as the child's parent in school when you are away. Some strategies that should be employed by the teacher and school management are extended time given to the child on assignments and tests, the child should be brought close to the teacher to avoid fidgeting, and this makes the child easily accessible to the ward should there be an emergency. Also, the use of graphs and chat is greatly encouraged. All these mechanisms ensure that the child feels supported and understood. It's also important you talk to your child about their diagnosis. This will help interrupt some of the stimuli they receive, like the urge to shout abruptly in class or make funny gestures that disrupt learning. This is particularly difficult as there may be an outburst of emotions between both parties (the parents and the child). However, some talking points could work as suggested by experts;

- Tell the child all there is about ADHD, including the symptoms, the medications, etc.
- Make them understand that they have a special brain. This could be done by letting them know that they have a type of brain that thinks fast and simultaneously, which could be distracting as they have many ideas simultaneously.
- Let the child know that their diagnosis is not a death sentence.
- Make the child feel they are not the only one with the condition. Show them statistics of people in the USA who have ADHD. Again, it's also smart to show them celebrities with ADHD. Celebrities like Michael Phelps, an Olympic champion in swimming; Simone Biles, a US Olympic champion in gymnastics; Justin Timberlake, a Grammy-winning singer, and actor; Adam Levine, a singer; Ty Pennington, a TV home repair guru; Terry Bradshaw, a super bowl champion to mention but a few. Knowing these will give them reasons to believe in themselves amidst the dysfunction and a sense of belonging.
- Inform your child about the recovery mechanism you intend to deploy, and always inform them when there is a change in the intended strategy. If your child is taking medications, don't criticize the drugs. This gives the child something to look forward to, making them feel carried along.

Now that you have earned your child's trust, it's best to look out for treatment plans. The treatment plan could be a pharmacological intervention or a non-pharmacological intervention. Examples of long-acting drugs are Dextroamphetamine (Adderall XR), Dexmethylphenidate (Focalin XR), Lisdexamfetamine (Vyvanse), and Methylphenidate. Therefore, there may be a need to take the stimulants multiple times a day. Research has shown that pharmacological intervention is essential in mitigating the effect of ADHD symptoms. These drugs help to improve ADHD symptoms. According to a study published by Lancet psychiatry, it states that it's "the easiest to tolerate and most effective option for an adolescent is methylphenidate (With brand names as Ritalin, Concerta, Daytrana, Aptensio XR, Metadate CD, and Methylin to mention a few.)".

Research suggests that using a drug as an intervention doesn't work 20% of the time. However, it is 80% effective. Parents or guardians are frequently concerned about the risk of addiction or abuse of drugs. However, researchers suggest offering child stimulants is better than leaving them to find one. This is the common cause of substance abuse amongst ADHD patients. The parent should oversee the administration of the drugs to their child to prevent substance abuse. Another commonly-raised worry by parents of patients with ADHD is that they are concerned about side effects from the medications. The Food and Drug Administration (FDA) recently authorized a medication that may be given throughout the night, and its effect is seen the following morning. This helps in giving the child an easy start for the morning. The name of this drug is Methylphenidate Hypochloride.

This drug is available to both adults and children with ADHD. The drug mentioned above could be effective and may elicit side effects. For adults, it may cause weight loss as the stimulant or drug reduces appetite, while it can lead to stunted growth for children. To mitigate these side effects, the parents or caregivers should proactively provide the adult or children with a healthy and balanced diet before taking their medications. The potential adverse effects include faster heart rate, higher blood pressure, and difficulty sleeping. It is also possible that one's personality may alter. According to Dr. Hallowell, stimulants are the golden standard. However, non-stimulant medication could be used when it doesn't work as it should. Non-stimulant increases the activities of the neurotransmitters that regulate attention. This neurotransmitter is called norepinephrine. This non-stimulant acts like stimulant drugs in short, intermediate, and long terms.

The notable side effects of non-stimulant are their ability to sedate a child and decrease blood pressure. There are treatment plans without medications in the management of ADHD patients. This is frequently called occupational therapy or non-pharmacological interventions for people with ADHD. Occupational therapy helps moderate the child's environment and brain interaction. It helps the child manage their own reflexes. Also, doing sporting activities could help the ADHD patient manage themselves well. During sporting activities, the child learns how to control themselves, reducing impulsivity, and the field becomes an outlet for them to express themselves energetically. Examples of such sports are horseback riding, soccer, swimming, and wall climbing, to mention but a few. Sporting activities elevate the level of neurotransmitters in the brain. Music therapy is very advantageous to an ADHD child. The music itself is soothing to the brain and relaxes the brain. This therapy stimulates the happy hormones that mediate memories and concentration. Playing musical instruments can be helpful too. This plays the same role as when someone plays the instrument for you. Also, arts such as painting, dancing, yoga, and singing could play a role in stimulating the rewards pathways, which helps relax the patient.

In conclusion, ADHD can be managed even though 30% of people diagnosed in childhood continue with it into adulthood. However, this fit comes with intentional practice, which may be overwhelming. It would help if you accepted your fate or your child's fate. Carry out a complete study of ADHD, as this could be done by reading academic articles on the subjects that are often available online or reaching out to a neuropsychologist for complete information on the dysfunction. This will help you make informed decisions as they arise.

2.3 Parenting Hacks for your Child's ADHD

Understanding Your Child's ADHD:
- Identify the Symptoms: ADHD varies among children, so knowing how it manifests in your child is essential. Focus on understanding your child's distracted, hyperactive, or impulsive stages and consult your therapist for the best approach tailored to your child's needs.
- Create Structure and Routine: Teach your child healthy habits by setting routines and encouraging self-care. Though it might take time, consistent effort will build their self-esteem and resilience.

Active Role in Treatment:
- Stay Engaged with Medical Care: Ensure your child follows their treatment plan, takes medication as prescribed, and consults with therapists regularly. Protect their medications and keep yourself informed about ADHD.
- Coordinate with School: Collaborate with your child's teachers to create a conducive learning environment tailored to their needs. Educate the teacher about ADHD if necessary.

Goal Setting and Expectations:
- Stay Engaged with Medical Care: Ensure your child follows their treatment plan, takes medication as prescribed, and consults with therapists regularly. Protect their medications and keep yourself informed about ADHD.
- Coordinate with School: Collaborate with your child's teachers to create a conducive learning environment tailored to their needs. Educate the teacher about ADHD if necessary.

Practical Strategies at Home:
- Stay Engaged with Medical Care: Ensure your child follows their treatment plan, takes medication as prescribed, and consults with therapists regularly. Protect their medications and keep yourself informed about ADHD.
- Coordinate with School: Collaborate with your child's teachers to create a conducive learning environment tailored to their needs. Educate the teacher about ADHD if necessary.

Maintaining a Positive Parent-Child Relationship:
- Spend Quality Time: Show love and support by engaging in activities, building trust and understanding.

- Self-Care for Parents: ADHD parenting can be overwhelming. Take care of your mental health to maintain a positive and supportive environment.

Avoid Common Pitfalls:

- o Stay Engaged with Medical Care: Ensure your child follows their treatment plan, takes medication as prescribed, and consults with therapists regularly. Protect their medications and keep yourself informed about ADHD.
- o Coordinate with School: Collaborate with your child's teachers to create a conducive learning environment tailored to their needs. Educate the teacher about ADHD if necessary.

Things NOT to Say to a Child with ADHD:

- o "Nobody needs to know you have ADHD."
- o "ADHD will stop when you are older."
- o "Having ADHD is not an excuse." (Instead, focus on understanding the underlying behavior.)

Summary:

Raising a child with ADHD requires empathy, patience, and consistency. The strategies outlined in this chapter offer a roadmap for navigating the challenges and joys of parenting a child with ADHD. Remember to prioritize self-care, seek professional guidance, and create a nurturing, disciplined environment.

In the management of ADHD in children, consider these principles:

- o Utilize Reward Systems: Recognize achievements and positive behavior.
- o Appropriate Punishments: If necessary, impose fair consequences aligned with the misbehavior.
- o Stay in Close Contact with Therapists: Regularly update your child's therapist and remember the medication schedule.

Remember, with the right strategies and support, children with ADHD can lead fulfilling lives. Your efforts as a parent are central to their success.

2.4 Strategies for managing a child with ADHD.

Managing a child with ADHD is a demanding and often overwhelming task. Understanding, patience, and empathy are key components in helping a child with this condition. Below, I'll outline some practical strategies that are not only specific to ADHD but also address areas that may not have been covered in other chapters of this book.

1. Be Calm; You're Not Alone: Recognizing that you are part of a larger community dealing with ADHD can be comforting. Focus on self-care practices that keep you mentally strong, such as taking breaks and finding support systems like informed caregivers.

2. Establish Flexible Rules of Conduct: Define clear and unambiguous rules for your child, emphasizing flexibility and consistency. Consider rewards for good behavior and consequences for mistakes, all balanced with understanding and patience.

3. Provide Opportunities for Exercise: Encourage physical activities that allow your child to focus on specific movements and enjoy sports. Running, climbing, gymnastics, karate, yoga, and skating are examples of activities that can positively impact coordination and reduce impulsivity.

4. Break Tasks into Manageable Chunks: Since focusing on large tasks may be overwhelming for a child with ADHD, breaking them down into smaller, manageable pieces can be helpful.

5. Collaborate with Teachers: Keep open communication with your child's teacher, informing them about the diagnosis and working together on strategies to reduce distractions and promote learning in the classroom.

6. Monitor Your Child's Diet: Ensure meals are balanced and avoid high-sugar or caffeine foods that might exacerbate symptoms. Consult with a pediatrician for specific dietary recommendations for ADHD.

7. Help Your Child Develop Social Skills: Actively teach social cues and encourage friendships by guiding their interactions.

8. Regulate Television Time and Encourage Active Engagement: Encourage activities that stimulate the mind and creativity instead of passive TV watching.

9. Incorporate Art into Regular Life: Utilize art and design in their environment to stimulate the brain and increase calmness.

10. Remember, Empathy is the Backbone: Always strive to be empathetic and avoid negative communication, as this could worsen the child's condition. Seek professional support if needed and focus on self-care to ensure you can provide the best possible care for your child.

By focusing on these strategies and integrating them with the parenting hacks, you can create a comprehensive and effective plan to support your child with ADHD. This chapter underscores the importance of adaptability, empathy, and collaboration in parenting a child with ADHD, focusing on unique strategies tailored to their specific needs and challenges.

2.5 How to improve your behavior toward your child with ADHD

Raising a child with ADHD requires understanding, empathy, and strategic adjustments in behavior. ADHD children's brains function differently, and as such, they exhibit unique behavioral traits. Here, we will explore ways parents can change their routine behavior to better meet the physical, mental, and emotional needs of their ADHD child.

Understanding ADHD

Before diving into strategies, it's essential to understand the underlying causes and characteristics of ADHD. This involves understanding medications, non-pharmacological interventions, behavioral management, and the specific symptoms listed by DSM-5 (refer to previous chapters for detailed information). Recognizing that your child's behavior is not willful but rather part of their condition can help prepare you to support them.

Intentional and Empathetic Parenting

Understanding that parenting an ADHD child can be stressful is crucial, but the task is worth the effort. Below are tailored strategies:

Organization and Structure:

- Break tasks into smaller, manageable chunks.
- Introduce consistent routines, allowing for adequate sleep and time for tasks.

Rewards and Consequences:

- Offer rewards for completed tasks and consider appropriate consequences ("cost of choice") for uncompleted ones. Balance this understanding of their condition.

Physical Activity:

- Encourage participation in sports or exercises they enjoy. Physical activity can help leverage their energy and improve motor skills.

Nutrition:

- Ensure proper meals and avoid substances like sugar and caffeine, affecting sleep and attentiveness.
- Pay special attention to food if your child is on medication, as some drugs have appetite-suppressing side effects.

Managing Fidgeting:

- Consider tools like weighted wraps or commercial fidget toys to reduce involuntary movements.

Social Skills Training:

- Teach turn-taking, public speaking etiquette, and respectful behavior. Practicing in real-life scenarios like park visits can be beneficial.
- Inform teachers and classmates of the diagnosis to foster understanding.

Emotional Support and Mental Health:

- Treat your child with empathy and compassion, fostering trust.
- Don't overlook your mental health; seek professional advice, take breaks, and ensure you have a supportive community.

The Case of Young Andre (Case Study)

Young Andre's case illustrates how ADHD impacts attention span and executive functions. This example can be referred to throughout the chapter to demonstrate the real-world implications of the strategies discussed.

Conclusion

Parenting an ADHD child can be challenging, but it's not insurmountable. Intentional and empathetic parenting, grounded in a robust understanding of ADHD, can help you guide your child through the complexities of their condition. Embrace a supportive community, professional advice, and treat your child with the compassion and understanding they deserve.

2.6 Managing the Relationship Between an ADHD Child and Siblings or Pets

This chapter is dedicated to understanding the intricate dynamics within a family where one child has ADHD. While parents of children with ADHD need to be well-informed to manage the condition, it's equally essential not to overlook the siblings. Let's explore how the presence of ADHD affects sibling relationships and provide guidance for families to navigate these challenges:

Understanding ADHD in the Family Context:

Ryan Williams is an 11-year-old diagnosed with ADHD. Like many children with ADHD, he exhibits articulate, loving, bright, and imaginative behaviors and impulsive tendencies. His actions often create conflicts with his siblings, leaving his family in a challenging situation. His mother's experience is a classical representation of how ADHD affects the entire family, including siblings and pets.

Rivalry at Home:

- Normalcy and Exaggeration: Sibling rivalry is a normal family dynamic. However, when a child with ADHD is involved, disagreements tend to be more frequent and taxing.
- Social Misjudgment: Children with ADHD may misjudge social situations, interrupt conversations, speak loudly, or act inappropriately. This can lead to embarrassment and exclusion.
- Attention and Resentment: The ADHD child often receives more attention, leading to resentment among siblings.

Support for Siblings:

- Recognize the Disorder: It is vital to help siblings recognize ADHD as a disorder rather than label the child as stubborn or attention-seeking.
- Avoid Negative Impact: How siblings perceive ADHD can be influenced by media messages and misconceptions. The correct understanding is key.

ADHD Sibling Support Strategies:

Here are practical ways you can support non-ADHD children in coping with the family dynamics:

- Balance Attention: Allocate dedicated time for non-ADHD children, ensuring they receive as much attention and nurturing as the ADHD child.
- Educate About the Condition: Make sure all children understand ADHD and its challenges. This includes explaining time management difficulties and controlling other symptoms.

- Collaborate with Non-ADHD Children: Work together to teach them how to handle problematic behaviors. Utilize strategies like brainstorming or role-playing to instill natural, loving responses.
- Empathize with Non-ADHD Siblings: If they have trouble handling ADHD siblings, be patient rather than reprimanding them quickly.
- Create an ADHD-Friendly Environment: Structure your home with specific routines, clear rules, consistent consequences, praise, and frequent feedback. This helps both the ADHD child and their siblings manage the complex dynamics.

This chapter aims to shed light on the multifaceted challenges and opportunities within families that include a child with ADHD. By understanding, empathizing, educating, and structuring the environment, parents can create a supportive atmosphere that nurtures all children in the family, regardless of whether they have ADHD. With patience, compassion, and knowledge, these challenges can be turned into opportunities for growth and connection for everyone in the family.

2.7 Learn to be empathic with your child.

Parenting a child with ADHD presents unique challenges and demands a nuanced approach. This requires a balance of understanding, empathy, and discipline to guide your child toward positive growth.

Understanding the Nature and Nurture of ADHD

The debate of nature versus nurture equally applies to children with ADHD. Nature refers to the genetic components transferred from parent to offspring, while nurture involves the environment's role, including social, cultural, and socioeconomic contexts. In the child's development, nature and nurture play significant roles, typically seen as a 50/50 influence on behavior.

Understanding this dynamic is crucial for ADHD parenting, as children across different cultures, locations, and socioeconomic levels will exhibit distinct behaviors. Therefore, there are no universal tips, but tailored strategies are necessary to nurture empathy and respect in children.

Goal Setting in Parenting

Your parenting journey should start with clear goals, asking questions like:

- What kind of parent do I want to be?
- What relationship do I want with my child?
- What values do I want to instill in my child?

These goals should be specific and actionable, considering the child's rights, health, and aspirations. The plans must be flexible, allowing children to explore the world and make informed decisions.

Redefining Discipline: Induction over Power Assertion

21st-century discipline often misconstrues the term's original meaning, leading to flawed corrective measures. Instead of acting impulsively and enforcing rigid punishments, discipline should aim to teach, instruct, and direct.

For ADHD children, discipline aims to foster independence, enabling them to choose between right and wrong. Effective discipline practices build empathy and connectedness, focusing on induction rather than power assertion.

Example: Discipline through Induction

Consider a scenario involving a child named Justin and his mother. After a promise of ice cream, Justin is disappointed to discover his mother bought the wrong flavor. In his impulsiveness, he drops the ice cream, making a mess.

Instead of reacting angrily, Justin's mom takes a moment to understand her child's feelings. She cleans the mess calmly, changes his clothes, and uses the opportunity to teach a valuable lesson about not wasting food. This response is called induction, a method where the parent appeals to a child's sense of empathy and values instead of using physical punishment.

In this way, Justin feels loved, and a connection is built, helping him learn a valuable lesson without resentment or fear. Induction, particularly for children with ADHD, builds a stronger, more empathic relationship, guiding them toward responsible behavior.

Conclusion

Empathy plays a pivotal role in raising a child with ADHD. Parents can build a nurturing environment by understanding the complex interplay of nature and nurture, setting clear goals, and redefining discipline. This environment helps foster respect, empathy, and self-discipline in the child, preparing them to become compassionate and responsible individuals. With dedication and a focus on induction over power assertion, parents can guide their ADHD child toward positive growth and development.

2.8 Parenting errors

Parenting is a complex and often challenging task, especially when navigating the unique needs and behaviors of a child with ADHD. It's essential to create a disciplinary approach that's individualized, consistent, and balanced. In this section, we'll identify common parenting errors and how to avoid them, aiming to nurture a positive and productive relationship with your child.

Short-term versus Long-term Discipline

Discipline should be more than just an immediate reaction to unwanted behavior; it should be a teaching tool that helps children understand the consequences of their actions in the long term. Immediate, short-term discipline might encourage children to be sneakier or to hide their actions. Focus on explaining why certain behaviors are unacceptable and what the long-term effects might be. This will help them understand and internalize the rules. Example: If a child continues to play soccer after being told not to, explain how it can affect other important activities like family time and academics. Show them that discipline isn't about punishment but about understanding and balance.

Consistency in Discipline

Children learn best when rules and consequences are consistent. Whether it's rewarding good behavior or penalizing the bad, make sure to follow through with what you've said. Inconsistency in discipline can undermine your child's trust and understanding of expectations.

Punishment versus Correction

While punishment can be an effective deterrent, it should never be the sole focus of discipline. The goal is to guide and correct behavior rather than merely penalize it. Punishments should be fair, loving, and aimed at helping the child grow and learn from their mistakes.

Alignment Between Parents

Both parents must be on the same page regarding disciplinary approaches. Misalignment can confuse the child and diminish the effectiveness of the discipline. Communicate openly with your partner and strive to agree on strategies that work for both of you.

Avoiding Toxic Comparison and Lies

Avoid comparing your child to others or lying about your past to motivate them. These tactics can damage self-esteem and create unnecessary pressure. Each child is unique and must be nurtured according to their needs and abilities.

Pseudo-discipline

Avoid using discipline to show off or prove a point to others. It can be harmful to your child's self-esteem and hinder genuine connection. Instead, focus on empathy and understanding, using methods that build trust and growth. Recommended Reading: "The Whole-Brain Child" offers insights into understanding how your child's brain functions and provides methods for improving connection, empathy, and relationship building.

Conclusion

Parenting a child with ADHD requires an extra layer of compassion, patience, and understanding. While there is no one-size-fits-all manual for parenting, avoiding common errors and applying the principles discussed here can foster a loving and supportive environment. Remember to be kind, affectionate, and flexible with your discipline approach, and always consider your child's age, development stages, and unique needs. The goal is to build a relationship that encourages empathy, growth, and responsible behavior at home and in the larger world.

3 MANAGING YOUR CHILD'S CONDITION

It is completely understandable that as a parent or the guardian of a child who has been diagnosed with ADHD, that you would sometimes feel short on patience and feel that you are overwhelmed. There is a certain amount of frustration that can be felt as a parent. However, this book was crafted as a guide to help you channel the ADHD of your child into a more positive channel. As a parent, you become the anchor of your child, to help them overcome whatever challenges they may encounter, redirect their energy into more fruitful and productive channels, and allow you to develop a level of control in your family. The earlier you are able to effectively manage your child's condition, the greater chances that you would have to manage your child in the years to come.

It was established in this book that the child who has been diagnosed with ADHD has an altered thought process wherein their executive function experiences deficits. It is expected then that those processes that enable them to develop plans, think ahead, organize themselves, control their impulses to act rashly, and ensure that a task you asked them to complete are missing. It is uncommon then to expect that your child would have bits of homework left undone, chores that were left incomplete, simply because something else was able to capture their attention more effectively. One of the more important roles that you can take on as a parent of a child diagnosed with ADHD then, is to be their anchor, the voice that tells them what they should do first, but not to the point that it has to all come from you. As the anchor of your child, it is necessary that you are able to let them develop their executive function and skills needed for them to properly function. A key idea to the management of the child with ADHD however, is that no matter how much they act out, their actions are not done willingly. They did not mean to make you lose your patience, frustrated or exasperated. They are unable to keep control of their own behavior. They want to be as organized, to sit quietly and remain behaved as much as you do, they just are unable to do so due to the altered perceptions that they sense. The most you can do is to support them in a positive manner, and exercise patience and compassion as you interact with them. They live in a mindset that they have no control of, it is up to you to assure them that you will always be there for them.

3.1. Positive Behaviors You Can Do

It is imperative that you are able to understand that ADHD would manifest in your child in so many different forms, which are naturally disruptive regardless of how they manifest. While you might think that your child is being willful in this case, it is more of a case that your child is unable to understand what you want them to do, or is unable to make themselves control their own behavior. They do have the tendency to be impulsive, in that they draw unwarranted attention upon themselves, and interrupt conversations to gain the wanted attention of their parent or from another person. If you happen to have other children who do not have ADHD, they in turn may be adversely affected with how your child with ADHD is handled, in that they may come to think that their needs are neglected in favor of the said child. Needless to say, that if the child thinks that acting out is the best solution to gain attention, that would be a recipe for disaster. That said, you need to develop the core values of compassion and consistency, in that your love for your child and how you treat them should take precedence over their own action, and that you should always be consistent. Be there for them, tell them that if a particular act is bad – that it is so that they may not repeat it.

1. It is important to take care of yourself first. As the parent or guardian of your child with ADHD, you remain the voice of reason by which your child is able to manifest their own executive functions. Ultimately it is how you manage yourself that is reflected in how you manage your child through their ADHD. It would not do well for your management skills if your child sees you about to break down or sob in front of them. No matter what you think, your child can sense that you are sad, and it makes them feel worse knowing that they might be the cause of it. Regardless of how hard, or how frustrated you must feel, it is important then to keep a positive attitude, not only for your child, but also for yourself. Once you are able to keep yourself calmed down, you will find that you are able to connect with your child and keep them calmed down as well.

   a. You may find mindfulness exercises useful for yourself, though recent studies that have utilized the same mindfulness exercises upon children diagnosed with ADHD have found that they too, are able to benefit from these mindfulness exercises, so this might be a common theme that you can take advantage of to further connect with your child.

   b. A different perspective helps. You might get tired of hearing this, but your child's behavior is not of their own free will. They love you too, and want to do right by you, so turn an act of your child into something hilarious that they can look back on

41

as they grow up. We see wholesome stories of children who scribble on walls. While some parents see this as a means to say redecorate a room, some parents also take the opportunity to put a frame around it and make it look like an art gallery. A sense of humor would greatly boost your spirits and that of your child.

c. Small steps help. The endgame of this book is to ensure that your child is able to function at their best. This book does not produce instantaneous results and as a result you will have to take some events as wins. If your child completed their homework, but left a chore undone, it's a good sign. It is pointless to expect perfection, more so from a child who was diagnosed with ADHD. Take and celebrate the small wins, for it is a sign that your child has at least developed an executive function that tells them that yes, homework can be done. There will be more time to develop other skills later on in life. There is no point in the added pressure, it will only make everything worse.

d. Believe in your child and in what they are capable of. Despite the erratic behaviors that can manifest in your child, they do have positive qualities that make you love and value them, and that make them unique. If they like to mess around with paints, you can call them artistic. If they like to sing, they can be musically gifted. Trust that your child will be able to gradually learn all what they need to over time, all you need to do is believe in them enough to ensure that it becomes so.

2. Care for yourself, there is no question about that. There is such a thing as caregiver exhaustion and this often manifests in families who experience little to no support in the care of their loved ones, in this context, you receive no reprieve from the care for your child. This is in line with your mental health care. If you become exhausted, you lose patience, and if you do that, you reset the progress you have made with your child.

a. Do not be afraid to seek help. The admission that you need help does not mean that you are a bad parent. It means that you are a good parent who understands that you might not be best for your child at the moment, and that you are strong enough to trust your child temporarily at least with another. There are centers that specialize in the care of children with ADHD. Obtain a recommendation from your physician, counselor or your child's teacher. Join support groups so that other parents may give you counsel and know what you can do better for your child.

b. Give yourself a break. There is no harm in that, provided that is, you do not overindulge in breaks too. It is perfectly fine to leave your child with family, friends, or even a daycare that specializes in the care of children with ADHD. It is important however, that you are able to explain certain routines and particular strategies that you employ should they act up. This way, you are able to find other people to rely on to help you care for your child, so you can care for yourself too.

c. Self-care cannot be stressed enough, so the more relaxed you are when you care for your child, the better you will feel too. Mindfulness exercises are best, as are exercises to help you sleep better. This way, you are able to care for yourself, physically and mentally.

3. Establish a structured routine. Children with ADHD thrive in structured environments because it allows them to predict and anticipate what the next routine will be every day. This also helps in the development of their executive functions, that they can also do it on their own through repetition.

a. Develop a routine for your child, and stick to it. It does not have to be elaborate however. It can be, wake up, shower, eat, school, pick-up from school, homework, play time, dinner, bed. Deviations from any structured routine are not ideal, as this would cause more opportunities for disruptive behavior to manifest in the child. When you set the routine however, it is best to involve your child in it. Let them lay out their school clothes for you, and make sure that items such as their schoolbag are kept in a handy place where they cannot forget about it.

b. Timers and alarms are a big help when you set a routine. Set times for when your child is supposed to accomplish a task that they were supposed to do. This helps reinforce the routinary behavior that brings structure to their lives. For instance, give them 30 minutes to an hour of homework (depending on how hard it is), then it would be dinner time. With the use of time, there is no point in acting like a drill sergeant. It only makes it worse. Use the timers and alarms judiciously, like 15 minutes of play before bedtime, and alarms to wake them up.

c. Scheduling remains a necessary skill, and it is best that in the establishment of a structured routine, that your child is able to utilize their time wisely. It is best that your child be kept occupied in accordance with their energy levels. Idle times where the child is not occupied only means that they have ample opportunity in which to manifest their erratic behavior. Hence, if your child has after school activities, some may require adjustments to ensure that your child is able to fully participate without any disruptions to the routine that you have established.

d. A quiet place for your child does wonders and this ensures that your child is able to have a safe and quiet space where they can do whatever they want. You can use a porch or a bedroom which has been fitted out with safety precautions. The only advise is that the quiet place is not the same place that you use to punish your children for their misbehaviors. This can cause them to develop negative connotations for their quiet place and impair their own sense of safety, which can also impair their behavior.

e. Organization starts from within, so you would have to step-up on your organization skills. It does not necessarily have to be a mixture of Marie Kondo plus all of those organization videos mind you, but it does have to be set up in such a way that your child understands that each object has a place that it should be in. Examples of this can be shoes in a mudroom, bag in a cubbyhole, clothes in the hamper and books on a shelf. The point here is that it encourages your child to develop the idea that each object belongs somewhere, and that they can help put the object in its proper place.

4. If your child is idle, it would be time perhaps to try a different approach. You can describe children with ADHD as those with excessive amounts of energy that need to be expended somewhere. A good strategy would be to sign your child up for after-school activities such as sports or art classes to help them use up their energy and to ensure that they have little idle time. This way, they are given lesser opportunities for their disruptive behavior to manifest, and are given activities that would occupy their attention.

a. In the same way, especially for weekends, Christmas and summer breaks in school, you can organize simple activities for your child. Bear in mind that these do not necessarily have to be chores however, as you want your child to be involved in the activity. Let your child help you prepare a meal, play a board game (it is advised that you do NOT give your child any video games or cellphone games as these are believed to be detrimental to the development of the executive function of your child.) You can also have them simply draw a picture, basically an activity that allows their time to be occupied and ensures that their attention is grabbed by an activity that employs thought.

5. It is no secret that children diagnosed with ADHD are full of energy, and it is a common strategy to help children burn through their energy through the use of physical activities and allow them to develop their focus on movements and particular skills. It is necessary to understand at this point that the use of physical activities is not limited to just burning up energy but the repetition that ensues allows for the development and improvement of the concentration of the child, lessens anxiety and allows the growth of the brain. A benefit here is that

once the energy levels of the child have been depleted, they are able to sleep more easily, which lessens the symptoms of ADHD.

    a. When you do choose an activity however, it is crucial that you select a sport that your child is interested in, and that involves minimal downtime (such as baseball and softball where the players are often kept in dugouts to wait their turn). Ideally, sports that produce a lot of movement such as basketball or hockey, or even martial arts and yoga are ideal. The latter two have an advantage in that it instills discipline along with the promotion of movement in the child.

    b. For bouts of spring fever, it is best that you provide time away from the screen of your phones and TVs. One of the rationales behind the reduction in screen time from phones and TVs is that they simply promote idle time and do not effectively occupy the attention of the child. Because they do not do so, they increase the likelihood of the disruptive behavior of the child to manifest. In this vein, it is necessary then to ensure that the child, their siblings, and yourself have some time away from the digital media and simply immerse yourself in nature. Bring them to a park, or the beach. This gives you the added benefit of having so many other objects that can occupy your child's attention and allows your child to burn off any excess energy they may have. As a parent, this also gives you the opportunity to relax while your children relax too.

6. Promote sleep. Most of us are quite cranky if we lack sleep, and you can imagine how much worse it is for a child who has ADHD and lacks sleep. If we are cranky, they are definitely higher up when it comes to the effects of sleep deprivation. It heightens the chances of the child to be very disruptive and that is the last thing that you want. They can be overstimulated as well, and that would be a bad thing. If you have employed the strategies outlined in the previous numbers, you will understand that the establishment of routine is crucial to this. If your child goes to bed by 8 or 9 pm, then be sure to stick to it. This is one strategy however, and there is more that can be done to ensure that your child is able to get a restful sleep.

    a. There is an established link between the amount of television time and the incidences of the symptoms of ADHD in a child. It is expected then that that television time be decreased or eliminated altogether if possible. While it is unknown as to why television exposure (and by extension any streaming app or video app that may be found on phones) increases the likelihood of the symptoms of ADHD, it may possibly be linked through overstimulation as provided by these aforementioned media. It is best though to have television viewing or other activities during the daytime as they are able to lower their energy levels by the time, they get to their set bedtime.

b. Caffeine levels should be reduced or eliminated. Needless to say, children should not be exposed to caffeine early, and children with ADHD should not be given caffeinated food and beverages early on given that caffeine is a stimulant, and children with ADHD have more stimulation than is actually needed. It may entail some sacrifice on your part, or preparation, but your child cannot have any soda, carbonated beverages (unless they are caffeine free), or even chocolate, as these are common sources of caffeine in food and drink. Similarly, what should be discussed in this section as well, is the amount of sugar that is taken in by the child, as food that is high in sugar can definitely elevate the activity level of the child. Processed foods with high amounts of sugar, to include prepacked fruit juice drinks should also be avoided in the diet of a child with ADHD then.

c. Transition periods or buffer periods are best utilized before your child is put to bed. This involves activities such as reading, coloring or quiet play. You do not want any activities that increase stimulation, so no video games, no competitive board games (so no Uno), no toys with flashing lights and no games that involve sound. Remember the goal here is to decrease activity, so your ultimate goal is to let your child relax by this time, at least an hour before bedtime when possible. At this point, you want to be more involved in your child care by cuddling your child and assuring them that you will be there for them. They feel secure in the knowledge that you are always there for them, and that you would watch them as they sleep. This will cause them to feel more relaxed and they can head to sleep faster.

d. Aromatherapy may help, as part of sleep hygiene for your child, and perhaps as well as for yourself. Soothing scents like lavender and mint would be nice as these exert a calming effect upon a child with ADHD, or even yourself. Try not to choose scents though that are evocative of food, you want calm and serenity, not hunger and cravings.

e. White noise generators are good if you can get them. If you cannot, you can always opt to play tapes of neutral sounds such as rainfalls to ensure that your child has some neutral background noise that can hopefully muffle any other sounds in their immediate environment. While there are available videos on white noise on video and streaming apps, they are not recommended simply because of the advertisements that tend to disrupt their continuity.

7. Structure and Routine are the cornerstone of the successful management of a child with ADHD. This entails a certain level of rigidity to ensure that your child is at least aware of limitations that have been set within the house. This does not give leeway however, to be harsh as a parent, even if this was done for the benefit of your child. Rigidity and consistency are crucial to ensure that your child is aware of expectations that are meant to be done at a particular time. This means then, that on weekdays, that your child is expected to be awake at a particular time. To avoid complications, it is best first to outline a simple set of rules that **everyone** can follow. It is important to stress that everyone should follow just to ensure consistency. It also assures the child with ADHD that the rules were not made because of them only in the long run. Make sure though that when you set the rules, they are easy enough for a child to understand. Do not use complicated language, and keep the rules short and simple enough. Let your child be able to see the rules so they can keep an eye on it. This helps bolster their development of consistency in what they do.

   a. At this point, it is necessary to elaborate on a rewards and consequences system, but not to the point that it becomes the sole basis by which your child behaves. Emphasize that if they are on their best behavior for a set period, they can say, go to the zoo, or visit their favorite place for one. If they break a rule, it is imperative that you do not resort to physical punishment on the child. This is not a book that sanctions any form of physical, emotional or psychological punishment. If your child does break a rule however, you can respond through it through the revocation of certain privileges – such as no TV in the daytime or some other activity that your child does. Be sure to toe the line carefully though.

   b. Do not be a perfectionist at this point. It is expected that children with ADHD are often criticized for their inability to remain consistent – something which is obviously beyond their control, and they are only doing what they can to cope. What can be done then is to reinforce positive behaviors. Give your child praise for the minor things, celebrate small wins. If they completed their homework, give them praise. Conversely, if they fail to do so, do not also immediately scold and criticize them. Be there for them, and help them through what needs to be done.

   c. Rewards, are a means to obtain positive reinforcement with your child, and it must be noted that rewards in this context does not entail material rewards, but rather praise and compliments, something that most children with ADHD rarely get given that they are constantly criticized and scolded, regardless of how watchful you are as a parent. It is important to note though, that you need to spice up your rewards a bit as the same type of reward for every good thing makes the reward repetitive, meaningless and boring despite your best intentions. As such, it is ideal that you can mix your material and non-material rewards carefully, provided they are able to effectively capture your child's attention. A good idea would be the use of a chart that shows the reward progression of your child, similar to how teachers use a star chart. It is entirely up to you however, how you want to disburse your rewards program, as long as you are consistent about it. Refrain from promises however, as they may be a source of disappointment for the child if left unfulfilled.

8. Mealtimes of the child with ADHD are similar to what a normal diet in children would entail. Normal, that is, being a relative term. By a balanced diet, this would entail a meal free from preservatives, made with fresh produce, and snack times that are free from junk food. Regular diets do not contain fast food, instant food or any type of food that one eats regularly. Your child then would need healthy, nutritious food, just like any other child. The difference is in the effect. For one, your child already has ADHD, therefore any food item that is high in sugar is guaranteed to ensure that your child has double the energy from not only their ADHD, but from the excess sugar that has entered their system. After the sugar rush, the child would most likely be irritable, and so will you after you have dealt with the inevitable sugar rush effects.

    a. One thing that you must take note of is that your child is always on a surge of energy that also boosts the rate at which their body consumes meals. Hence, it is expected that your child will eat more frequently than average. There is also a high chance that because of their high distractibility, your child may also forget to eat, not finish their meals, or subsequently over eat, hence accommodations would have to be made for portions that your child will not take long to consume, preferably with snacks that are sugar-free.

    b. Your child may be hungry but do not expect them to adhere to regular meal time schedules despite our stance on the importance of a schedule. This does not mean however, that you should only permit your child to eat three meals plus snacks each day, no. This involves spacing the frequency of the meals at least three hours apart to ensure that your child at least is able to get the nutrition that they need without the need to burn up all of the calories that they were able to use up throughout the day.

    c. Meal times are to be encouraged and make sure they form part of the regular routine of your child. The substance of your meals though should be as freshly-prepared as possible. This means no fast food -given the high-fat and high-sugar content of the entire menu. There should be no junk food in the house (but since junk food is a guilty pleasure after all – be sure to at least hide it properly and make sure your child does not see it, out of sight, out of mind). In addition to this, television advertisements that advertise junk food and fast food should be avoided, and to be safe, provide your child with a vitamin and mineral supplement – ask your pediatrician to provide you with a prescription that is compatible with your child's medication.

9. The last positive step that you can do as a parent is to socialize. Your child may find it hard to make friends as they find it hard to understand social cues, they may talk too much, interrupt conversations between others, or be thought of as too aggressive in their approach to people. Aggression in this case should not be thought of as violent behavior, but rather, the type of aggressiveness you would associate with a telemarketer who persists on making contact even though you would rather not deal with their product.

a. Your child will definitely require instructions, but it is important to ensure them that there is nothing wrong with the way they act, but there are some changes that can be done to ensure they make friends more easily. Tell your child that they need to know how to understand people (read faces is more like it, but this might be taken literally).

b. Your child will encounter challenges as not everyone would want to be their friend. This is one thing that you would have to make sure your child understands to ensure that they are at least aware that people do not become friends immediately.

c. Role-play is always a good idea. Not only does it give you more time to bond with your child but it also gives them the opportunity to learn how to act in different situations. You might want to start with proper ways to introduce yourself, what to do when you meet someone new, and what you can do that is friendly.

d. Your child has their own needs, and much as you would hate to be cliquish, there is no other option but to ensure that your child plays with playmates who are safe for them. Be selective in your child's friends. If they happen to be aggressive, then keep them away from your child. Make sure that your child's playmate is someone who is able to communicate at the same level as your child, and is able to move at the same level your child can.

e. It would be appropriate to test limits out with regards to socialization. Needless to say it is a bad idea to invite the whole class over as this can lead to overstimulation. Invite one or two friends of your child over to the house for a structured playtime. Be sure that they are able to engage in safe play and absolutely forbid instances of pushing, hitting and yelling.

These three behaviors are red flags that indicate that they are not the best friends for your child to play with – or friends for that matter.

    f.   Provide time and a space for your child to play. Even playing alone would be alright (except if it is video games or even mobile games) and if your child is able to play by themselves, and they are able to do it well enough, be sure to reward them for good behavior. Good play behavior would involve, for one, no video games and computer games, or even mobile games, and two, if they are able to arrange their toys afterwards, or if they are with friends or siblings, they did not throw a tantrum, those things are to be positively rewarded.

3.2. How You Are Reinforcing Negative Behavior Without Even Knowing It

As parents, our intentions are typically filled with love and concern for our children. We wish to see them flourish and excel in their endeavors, and naturally, we feel we have to guide, nurture, and protect them. But do our actions sometimes inadvertently lead to the reinforcement of negative behavior? The unsettling reality is that we, imperfect humans, may inadvertently expose our children to unhealthy attitudes and behaviors, even with the purest intentions. This chapter examines how this might occur:

1. Modeling Behavior: Children are skilled observers. They often mimic what they see, hear, or perceive. For example, a child growing up in an environment where parents lack respect for each other may unintentionally learn to display disrespect towards others.

2. Failing to Correct Misbehavior: Allowing children to continue negative behaviors without correction reinforces those behaviors. If a child is not gently corrected with love when they act inappropriately—such as taking things that don't belong to them—we may inadvertently encourage that behavior.

3. Instilling Fear Through Harsh Correction: When we raise our voices or react harshly, we might foster a fear of expression in our children, hindering their ability to communicate and assert themselves in difficult situations.

5. Encouraging Envy or Imposter Syndrome: Comparing children to others may inadvertently foster feelings of inadequacy or envy. Children may feel they can never measure up, leading to a long-term struggle with self-esteem.

6. Body Shaming: Comments about appearance, even if meant as encouragement to eat healthily or exercise, can have long-lasting, damaging effects. Such remarks may seem harmless but can take a significant emotional toll.

Conclusion

As parents devoted to our children's welfare, we must be mindful of how our behavior and words might be interpreted. While our intentions may be pure, it's crucial to recognize that we might inadvertently cause harm. By being aware of these potential pitfalls, we can strive to parent in a more understanding and empathetic manner, promoting positive growth and development.

3.3 The big question is - Can parenting affect ADHD?

Parenting a child with ADHD can present unique challenges, and while parenting itself does not cause ADHD, it plays a significant role in managing the disorder. The relationship between parenting and ADHD can be explored through the following areas:

1. Avoid Negative Communication: Your child's ADHD should not diminish your love and care. Treating all children with respect and empathy is crucial, regardless of their condition. Negative comments can have lasting effects and should be avoided.

2. Focus on Strengths Rather Than Weaknesses: Children with ADHD may struggle with concentration and focus. Instead of emphasizing their shortcomings, highlight their strengths. Encourage and nurture their abilities, offering support to improve areas where they face difficulties.

3. Avoid Comparisons with Others: Comparing children with ADHD to their peers may lead to feelings of inadequacy. Patience and intentional guidance are needed for their growth, even if progress seems slow.

4. Set Reasonable Expectations: Children with ADHD may require reminders and clear instructions. Avoid imposing unrealistic or unachievable expectations, recognizing that, like all children, they might need constant guidance. Tailor your expectations to their individual abilities and needs.

5. Spend Quality Time Together: Accepting a diagnosis of ADHD can be overwhelming, but your child needs your attention more than ever.

Foster a loving and supportive home environment to ease their connection with the broader world.

6.   Educate Yourself About ADHD: Understanding ADHD is vital to effective parenting. Engage with treatment plans, administer medications responsibly, and secure them properly. This knowledge will guide you in supporting your child's unique needs.

7.   Seek Support When Needed: Parenting a child with ADHD can be exhausting and stressful. Don't hesitate to seek support from communities or groups of parents who understand your situation. Sharing experiences and strategies can be a valuable source of encouragement and learning.

Conclusion:

Parenting does not cause ADHD, but how we parent can significantly influence a child's disorder experience. Adopting positive strategies and avoiding common pitfalls can provide a nurturing environment that helps your child thrive. Your child's journey with ADHD doesn't have to be faced alone; resources, communities, and professional guidance are available to support you and your child.

3.4 Managing ADHD at Home and at School

There are no bones about the fact that it takes a lot of people in concert to raise a child diagnosed with ADHD. Much as you would want to do it on your own, seeking help does not mean that you are a bad parent. It means that you understand that you are in a position that requires additional help and that you understand that this would be for the benefit of your child. At this time, your child travels between two constant environments, home and school. It is these milieus that are essential in the establishment of effective management strategies in a child who was diagnosed with ADHD. As such, there are certain strategies that can be employed by parents and teachers to effectively manage the symptoms of ADHD that manifest in the child.

Regardless of how meticulous you effectively manage your child's symptoms, there are instances however where no matter how watchful you are with your child, the symptoms of ADHD would still manifest. This is another constant that you would need to watch for. A 2020 study written in the Clinical Child and Family Psychology Review narrates a method referred to as Behavioral Parent and Teacher Training (BPT). This is a method more commonly utilized by parents and teachers who wish to utilize a non-pharmacological based approach in the management of the symptoms of ADHD in a child.

As a parent, you have the option to choose non-pharmacological methods to manage the symptoms of ADHD in your child. While there are pharmacological means to manage these symptoms, there are bound to be side effects that can arise with the prolonged dependence on the medications that were mentioned in this book. That said, it is also important to note that one has to strike a balance between the two, in that effective management of the symptoms must employ both judicious application of pharmacologic and non-pharmacologic options. One cannot wholly be reliant on just one method of management, hence, while the child has part of their symptoms managed by the use of the medications prescribed to them, effective management can be augmented through the use of the PBT.

Behavioral Parent and Teacher Training is known to reduce oppositional behaviors, improve your quality of positive parenting while it conversely reduces incidences of negative parenting, and increases the sense of competence with parents. Expected outcomes can include your child who listens to you more, and provides you with more opportunities to reward them for their good behavior, with due consideration to the precepts that involve the proper reward for such an occasion and a reduction of negative parenting behaviors and punishments inflicted upon the child.

The core topic then, of method revolves around the use of instrumental learning principles where the parents of the child and the teachers involved in the care of the child are taught about the reinforcement of non-adaptive behavior firstly. This means that the child should understand that if they misbehave in any place that is out of the home for one, there are consequences. As is the case, there must be a line drawn between the use of harsh and corporal punishments in contrast to other forms of punishment. The punishments in this case should not adversely affect the child. The parents and teacher are also taught to anticipate cues and behaviors that can determine if a child is about to engage in these types of behavior. While the whole concept is effective, it has to adapt as the child takes on newer behaviors that can be manifested through other means. This method however is heavily reliant on the use of reward and punishment of the child and hence, can be perceived to be outdated by most parents.

The main basis for the treatment and psycho-education for parents and teachers who have children diagnosed with ADHD is reliant upon the use of education on the part of the parents. We will not delve into that further, as it is understandable that you have done your part as a parent to learn more about how you can help your child better manage their condition. That aside, it is not enough that you know solely about how the mind of a child with ADHD functions. There is no point in learning about the pathophysiology as there is none to learn about. It is important then, to help your child integrate into society and enable them to function to the best of their abilities and ensure that their behavior remains acceptable or at the least they are able to show a modicum of control over the need to engage in their more impulsive behaviors.

Instrumental learning is another strategy that is employed to help in the management of the symptoms of ADHD in a child. It is defined as an observable change in the behavior of a child due to the application of the concepts of reward or punishment onto the behavior of the child. For instrumental learning to be successful however, it is a prerequisite that the child understands which types of behaviors lead to the reward, and which behaviors lead to consequences. It is this behavioral stimulus that leads to the Dynamic Developmental Theory. Recall that your child, regardless if they have ADHD or not needs attention and that they would act out to get any kind of attention, even if it is negative. That would be a constant in a psychological approach. Now, the child who does not have ADHD would quickly understand that some behaviors are deemed unacceptable and some behaviors are perfectly fine to get the attention that they need. The child with ADHD does not immediately grasp that yet, and hence there is the need for constant reinforcement to show them that certain behaviors lead to rewards, and that maladaptive forms of behavior lead to consequences. It is at this point also, that as a parent, that you would be more effusive with your rewards. Your child wants your attention more than they want a material object. The theory and hence the instrumental learning hinge upon the child's ability to understand the behaviors that can reward or punish them, and the consistency of your approach. It would not do well to ignore your child if you are busy, as they will interpret this as a means to test out their boundaries more, which would lead to more instances of disruptive behavior. The more quickly you respond to their behavior, the quicker your child will understand that their act is either wrong (and would result in consequences), or correct (and results in a reward for their behavior). Conversely, if you are lenient or slow to react to their behaviors, your child would then also take some time to understand which behaviors are best suited and which behaviors are inappropriate in any setting.

Raising a child takes effort and understanding, and parenting a child with ADHD presents additional challenges. However, these challenges can be navigated with empathy and the right information. Here's how:

At Home

1. Understand Your Child's ADHD: ADHD affects the prefrontal cortex, impairing functions like planning and focus. Recognize specific problems and develop supportive structures tailored to your child.

2. Build Empathetic and Flexible Plans: Break tasks into manageable pieces and approach your child with warmth and patience. Make room for mistakes, understanding that behaviors are not willful but a part of ADHD.

3. Create Consistent Expectations and Rewards: Develop a system of consistent expectations, rewards, and discipline across all caregivers to help your child understand consequences.

4. Encourage Physical Activities: Sports like martial arts or basketball can teach self-control and patience, while group activities enhance social skills.

5. Use a Planner: Help your child stay focused by breaking activities into smaller chunks. Planners help in managing time and maintaining focus on tasks.

6. Mind Your Own Wellbeing: Caregiving can be stressful. Seek help when needed and find ways to relax and recharge.

In School

Children with ADHD require a different set-up, but not a different environment away from the friends that they have made over the years. The school remains the second home of your child, and the teachers are in the position of surrogate parents while the child is in the classroom. This means that the development of your child may progress or may be stalled depending on the approach that the teacher uses, hence teachers who handle students with ADHD do need to be aware of methodologies to better manage the child who has ADHD. This section however, is not limited to only teachers but also teacher's assistants who would be a great help to prepare and set up the environment and activities for your child.

For the teacher and the teacher's assistant, there are certain expectations that must be set, if you haven't had time to go through the entire book. The child with ADHD is by no means slow, but does have a hard time with executive decisions that tell the child when they are to stop. It is necessary to remain constant and firm in your approach with them, and be aware of the need for an effective reward and consequence system – much in the same way that you would tell a rambunctious child to go to the time out corner in your classroom.

First, your child will definitely be impulsive – this means that they are most likely to interrupt conversations (such as your lectures and activities), act before they think and are generally unaware of the danger that surrounds them. This does take some time to get used to, but it must be noted that it would be pointless to yell at the child or be harsh.

Your child will be hyperactive, it is in the name after all. Hence your child will be unable to sit still, or if they are sitting down – fidget constantly, and have excessive movements. In this instance, you would have to ensure that your immediate environment is safe and child-proof to minimize the risk of injury that the child may incur while they are in their hyperactive episode. This would take some time to come to terms with however, but over time the child will get accustomed to the rules provided you follow the same reward and consequence strategy the parents of the child employ. Ask the parents how they do it, so you can ensure consistent application throughout the school and the home.

Inattentiveness is another key trait, where given that attention deficit is in the name of ADHD, it is expected then that your child would be highly distractible due to a short attention span. You will find that they are unable to devote a lot of attention to tasks, or shift from task to task constantly as the current task that they were previously on did not sufficiently capture their attention (through no fault of your own). You would generally observe the signs that show that a child has been inattentive through the movements and behaviors that the child has exhibited.

There are a few steps that the parent and teacher can undertake to ensure a more harmonious relationship to effectively manage the ADHD of any child.

1. Establish a Connection with School Staff: This works vice versa where you as a parent can develop a relationship with your teacher and school, and for teachers to develop closer working relationships with other professionals who can help maximize the learning that your child with ADHD does. Here, as a parent, you can work with teachers, counselors, and psychologists to understand your child's needs in the educational environment. Teachers on the other hand, would also need to work with other professionals to ensure that the teaching pedagogies employed would be suitable for the developmental level of the child and ensure that the material and activities provided to them are appropriate for the child.

2. Know your Child – This provides opportunities to know more about your child. Ideally, this would be done at a period before your child starts a new class to ensure that they are able to adjust accordingly. Parents in turn, can initiate this for the teacher if the teacher is new, and together, you can make a list about your child. What do you feel that your child is strong at, and where can the teacher make improvements to highlight those skills. Similarly, you can also highlight weak points in your child's behavioral set up and ensure that your child's teacher is aware of any weaknesses that they may be able to better address in a classroom set up. This should not be a one-off communication however, as it would be beneficial to both parties concerned to communicate with each other over the progress of your child.

3. Educate Classmates: Informing classmates about ADHD can foster a compassionate and supportive atmosphere. This would be an approach that can potentially work if applied properly. Your goal here is not

single out the developmental differences in your child, but to ensure that their classmates are aware of their needs and to not take offense with any inappropriate behaviors that are exhibited. That said, this approach would fare better if the child has other friends who are aware of their developmental skills and levels and they would be able to ease the way for a smoother integration into the classroom population. While the education process takes place, it would be best to ensure that you employ the same zero-tolerance policy parents to: No to hitting, teasing, pushing or screaming. For additional involvement, you must ensure that the educational portion for ADHD is framed in such a way that you ensure that there is no chance for bullying. If possible, let your child be involved and allow them to explain to their classmates what it would be like for them.

4. Create an ADHD-Friendly Environment: Protect the child from distractions, communicate with visuals, and use fidget tools if they help. This goes beyond the pedagogies that you employ as a teacher, as the safety of the child remains a paramount concern within the classroom. Given that the ability of the child to sense danger is inhibited or simply unlearned, you would have to ensure that most containers are child-proof, corners are softened, pathways are clear of debris and so on. This will definitely get your hands full, so it is best that you request assistance, when possible, to ensure safety of your child. It would also be best to avoid time-based tests as this can cause the child to worry excessively and display a tantrum that you might find it hard to overcome.

5. Structure Tasks and Allow Extra Time: Break down assignments into manageable steps and provide additional time for quizzes or assignments. A more effective arrangement in seating would include placing the child closer to you to ensure that you are able to monitor them more closely. If this is not possible, then you can seat the child in an area where there are no distractions, such as away from doors, windows and perhaps, your most talkative students. Though it may seem to be a good idea to place your student with their friend, this would only serve as a distraction. You would have to observe however, and if the student benefits more from having their friend close by, then you may seat the child next to them. You may also sit the child close to the pencil sharpener and the trash bin, so that in case they do need to expend their energy, they can do it through sharpening their pencil. Be sure to have someone watching at least so they do not poke themselves or another person with the pointed end.

6. Utilize Positive Reinforcement: Rewarding good behavior and focusing on strengths can boost confidence and encourage progress. The rewards in this case, do not have to be material, but you do need to ensure that not only does the child with ADHD gets rewards, but also the rest of the class to ensure equal treatment and prevent instances of bullying due to the special circumstances. You may be familiar with the use of a star chart or a points system arrangement to ensure that your child is encouraged to exhibit more positive behaviors and is rewarded for it.

7. Establish Rules and a Routine – you should get your cues from your child's parents, and the structure of the routine of the child in school should at least follow the one they have from home, particularly when it comes to meal times. That aside, what needs to be addressed here is the establishment of rules first. Ideally, you should get your students' input on these rules, and they must be written in such a way that the rules are more positive in their approach. Tell them what you want them to do once they enter your classroom as opposed to what they should not do. Hence, it is important that rules such as "Once in the classroom, put your bag in the cubbyhole and sit properly" be made, rather than "Do not make noise". The rules have to be short though, to at least make them easier to understand. When you set the rules and the routine in your classroom, be sure to first get the attention of your child with ADHD. This would take some time, so a lot of patience and repetition may be needed given their short attention span. Eye contact is more useful in this instance as this shows that you want the child's attention more. You can reinforce these rules and routines through visual cues around the classroom such as posters of the rules and routines in various places in the classroom.

8. Break Down Tasks – this is a strategy that can be employed by both parents and teachers. You can recall the sensation when a project or lesson seems to heavy and complicated when you first hear of it, but it becomes easier once it has been broken down into more manageable sections. This same approach can be employed for your child with ADHD. While the tenets of this book show consistency, with the learning materials, in this case, it would do to have some variety to ensure that the attention of your child would be effectively captured regardless of the method and they would be able to learn their lessons at the same time. A good idea would be to have workbooks, interactive games, and electronic devices (only for learning- never for entertainment purposes), as these are surefire ways to get a child's attention and allow them to focus on the lesson. For teachers, it is a

must to give homework and time extensions to the child with ADHD, and ensure that the homework given to them is formatted in such a way that it has sufficient interest or at least is broken down into step-by-step instructions that are easy enough for the child to accomplish. Give them enough time as well to complete tests.

Conclusion

Managing a child with ADHD requires collaboration and understanding among parents, school staff, friends, and family. With clear communication, structure, empathy, and positive reinforcement, you can support your child in developing skills that will help them thrive in school, work, and relationships. It's not about changing the child's behavior but about adapting the environment and our approaches to suit their unique needs. By doing so, we facilitate their growth and enrich our lives along with theirs.

3.5 Social Skills Therapy Techniques

ADHD symptoms can profoundly affect social skills. Individuals with ADHD often struggle with relating to peers and maintaining relationships because of their frequent inattentiveness, impulsivity, and hyperactivity. They may have difficulty taking turns in conversations or shared activities. These social skills, essential for effective communication, become even more vital when we consider their impact on a person's mental well-being and self-esteem.

Understanding Social Skills

Social skills encompass behaviors that aid in understanding and responding to verbal and non-verbal cues when interacting with others. An inability to socialize can lead to loneliness, potentially leading to negative behaviors like joining detrimental groups. Some essential social skills include:

- Establishing eye contact
- Recognizing when a conversation partner wants to change the subject
- Expressing opinions appropriately
- Listening actively to others
- Sharing in others' emotions (laughing when they laugh, showing empathy when they're upset)
- Initiating and maintaining conversations

These skills contribute to a person's social competence. ADHD can threaten these abilities, causing individuals to act impulsively or appear hyperactive in social situations.

Improving Social Skills in ADHD Children

Here are some practical strategies to foster social skills in ADHD children:

- Teach Conflict Resolution: Educate your child on how to respond to conflicts with peers, emphasizing appropriate avenues like seeking help from a teacher.
- Understand Social Rules: Social skills vary among cultures and locations, so help your child consciously learn and practice the social rules applicable to their community.
- Encourage Interaction with Diverse Groups: Expose them to people from different backgrounds, broadening their understanding of the world.
- Utilize Teachers: Teachers can boost an ADHD child's self-esteem through classroom activities and targeted support.
- Pair with Compassionate Peers: This approach can be highly effective, as illustrated by Russell's case. Russell, a child diagnosed with ADHD, was paired with a trained buddy, James, leading to a significant improvement in social skills and confidence.
- Be a Role Model: As a parent, exemplify the essential social skills your child needs to develop, fostering trust and resilience.
- Engage in Roleplaying: This technique helps children hone their communication skills and can be deployed at home and in the classroom. For example, Danielle, a 5-year-old child, learned valuable life lessons through role-play with her counselor after a classroom conflict.
- Facilitate Small Group Playdates: Monitor and correct behaviors during playdates with small groups, noting how your child interacts and how others respond.
- Provide Feedback: Clear, consistent feedback helps your child understand their social miscues and how to improve.
- Foster Self-Awareness: Teach your child to recognize how their actions affect others and emphasize the importance of social awareness in building friendships.

Structured Group Play

You can hardly call it socialization if your child does not have anyone else to socialize with. However, as it was stressed in the previous sections of this book, that you cannot simply place your child into a group and assume that they would be readily accepted as a playmate. While it would be nice to believe that your child will be readily accepted, to be perfectly frank, you would have to exercise control over whom your child can safely play with. It must be reiterated then that children who act like bullies, who push, scream, yell and perform similar actions are definitely not ideal playmates for your child and should not be considered at all for this type of parental strategy for socialization.

You want an environment where your child feels safe enough to play as themselves, with supervision by you or a trusted parent or friend. Now, you might get the idea that this is the concept behind structured group play. This is just part of it, as the entire idea encompasses that of any activity or game wherein toddlers and preschoolers (for whom this approach is specifically designed for), to develop executive functions such as sharing, learning how to take turns, and counting from one to three. This type of structure is indeed, best done under the guidance of a parent, a teacher or an approved caregiver.

Not all games fit the notions of structured group play, as you want the games under this to include some form of subliminal instruction that allows your child to learn while at the same time expend their excess energy. Hence, more simplistic games such as catch and throw would allow them to develop motor skills and improve hand-eye coordination; Simple Simon (Simon Says), allows the child to learn how to follow instructions; and board games – which teaches the child to take turns – Snakes and ladders or Chutes and Ladders would be a great game are ideal games with which to start off your structured group play. For older children, structured play may work, but it would be advisable to stick to board games where the movements are more apparent. Card games are somewhat advisable, given that some of them are rather complex in their rules – even Pokémon cards (though admittedly these will at least capture their attention effectively). That aside, some games like Uno – with its visual cues and bright colors make taking turns more fun; Egyptian War – though you would have to watch out for any violent reactions; Go Fish – a classic, would be also great as this allows not only the development of the skill of taking turns, but also improves the memory and ability of the child to concentrate. As with most games, however, it does take some time to teach the rules to your child with ADHD, therefore a lot of patience is needed to ensure that they grasp the rules that are needed to properly play any game, not just the card games.

There are other alternative activities that you can use as part of the structured group play though. Swimming may be made part of a structured group play, provided the appropriate safety measures have been taken, or you can simply use an inflatable kiddie pool to avoid most mishaps. There are benefits to swimming as extolled by Michael Phelps, the Olympian who himself was diagnosed with ADHD. Swimming as an activity is believed to lessen the need for ADHD Medications (though you will want to confer with your pediatrician for this). You will need medications still for more cognitive functions that allow your child to read and write more effectively, the effect would stem however, from the lessened need for stimulation in a child who swims as the activity gives them enough stimulation to be alert and focused on the activity. The added advantage with swimming is that the child would expend a lot of excess energy and does not give them enough energy to engage in more inappropriate behaviors. Swimming as an activity contains enough repetitive movements and structure that requires your child to devote as much focus as they possibly can, and are simple enough that your child will not have a hard time following instructions. It also helps that swimming itself exposes your child to several forms of stimulation, such as the sight of the pool, the sound of splashing water, the feel of water on their skin, which help counteract the tendency of their brain to be hyperactive and act inappropriately due to a lack of attention – as the child would have to focus on themselves.

Music and Dance can also be other ways to engage in group play, to add some variety to the routine. Remember that children can be easily bored, more so if they have ADHD, hence, you do need some variety to add some fun to their routine. A good way to do this would be through music and dance, again, provided the appropriate safety measures have been taken such as rubber puzzle mats and pillows in case the child loses their balance. Music has been shown to develop an emotional connection with a person, and you as a parent can recall that, particularly when you have a favorite song that you can play on YouTube at any moment, the same goes for your child. The use of music in this instance does not only entail music already made by artists, your child can also learn how to play an instrument or dance. This gives your child the opportunity to be fixated on activities that are positive and allows their attention to be captured more effectively. While some children may take to learning musical instruments – the piano and the violin are good examples, some children may prefer other forms of expression through music, which is why dance is included in this discussion. The structured routine and repetitive movements and rhythms required in these activities answer the desire of the child to have attention focused solely onto them. Because the attention of the adult is focused on the child, the child in turn will want to do the activity that holds the attention of the adult. Aside from this, the new information and sensory stimulation from the use of instruments and dance allows the child's attention span to be captivated more. For a start, you can have your child involved in the creation of a favored playlist that they enjoy as this allows your child to focus on the task to determine what kind of music they actually like. Once they have done that, you can simply add this onto a CD (if you still use them), or make an updated playlist on YouTube or Spotify exclusively for them. This also doubles as a project that you can reward your child for, as they were able to successfully complete it. This would also benefit you as a parent on days when your child feels unmotivated. The right song, preferably a rhythmic one, would provide sufficient motivation for your child to get moving, and allow them to focus on getting ready for the day's activities. Do not forget to reward them for that. Now, we get to the part where this becomes integral to structured group play, throw a dance party. You can come up with themed dance parties to make it more fun for your child and ensure that they are able to focus on the activity and enjoy the company of approved friends. This way, they are able to expend all of their extra energy in the company of friends in a controlled situation that you are able to supervise with the help of a friend or parent. It is stressed that you do not do these types of activities as a lone adult.

For the child who prefers to work indoors, you can opt to stage a structured group play around arts and crafts. This type of activity allows your child to exercise their creativity and develop their executive thinking abilities to focus and express themselves with other children who are in their friends list (not to sound cliquish). The advantage with arts and crafts is that this allows your child to be more self-directed, in that they are able to set a direction for themselves in how they want to continue. This is something that they cannot get from team sports as this requires rapid thinking often times on their own. The self-direction that they can get allows them to express their individuality and work towards their own goal. If your child wants to build a house made of popsicle sticks, this will allow them to work towards that, or if they want to make a bakery out of modelling clay (be careful with this), or simply if they want to draw a picture. Because the use of arts and crafts employs multiple senses, this gives them enough sensory stimulation to allow them to focus on the task at hand. This in turn captures their attention and gives them an outlet for their energies to be expressed. A good after school activity may be art classes, or you can simply arrange for your child to color and share with their friends.

Great activities that can be included under this include painting, especially paint by number kits, coloring books, science experiments (though any kits with these should only be used under adult supervision and if the appropriate safety precautions have been taken), and origami (paper folding, but with simpler figures).

These are just some of the activities that you can undertake under structured group play. While the notion of play may indicate idle time for your child to not do anything, this runs contrary to our perception of play. Playtime, in general, provides opportunities for personal, social and emotional development, which are necessary in the proper development of a child who has ADHD, as well as for other children. Without the use of structured playtime, preschoolers and toddlers may have a more difficult time in the development of executive thinking skills, socialization and physical and mentally develop. The use of structured group play also allows you to engage your child in other types of activities that they would normally be unable to do on their own. While the aforementioned activities are favorable for the children, it is best to start them off slowly, say, thirty minutes, just to see how it goes. Over time, you can gradually increase the time spent in structured group play and structure it around the interests of your child.

You would have to tailor the activities to the age of your child, as most of these activities are geared towards children who are in kindergarten or early elementary (Grades 1 to 3). Babies for instance, may benefit from a simple activity of peek-a-boo to help develop their object permanence, which normally develops in a child about 5 months. Do this only when your baby is well-rested as the child can be easily irritated. If they are, give it a break and try again later. You may also opt to read to your child to ensure that your child gets accustomed to your voice, and though they cannot say it yet, they will gradually come to understand the tone of your voice, and how you say it, and how it makes them feel. They would be able to understand if you are happy, sad, loving, and all other forms of emotion. Babies who were read to were shown in studies to have better vocabularies and math skills later on in life. This can perhaps be attributed to the early influence of reading material on them. With your tone of voice, your child will later on be able to pick up on emotions in your voice and tell if you are happy or sad or angry. A last recommended activity is the use of building blocks, which coincidentally make a great activity for structured group play as it allows your child to develop the trait of sharing with other children and learning to work as part of a team (though do not expect complicated results, they are children after all). This also allows your child to express their creativity in what they do, despite its relative simplicity.

For the school-aged child and toddlers, there are those activities such as swimming, arts and crafts and music and dancing that can effectively occupy their time properly if spaced correctly and done with the proper supervision. If you do want some additional variety however, to what they want to do, you can also opt to stage fake plays and puppet shows. The materials and costumes do not have to be expensive mind you, but this allows the execution of several things. For one, since there is physical movement involved, you can be assured that your child will be able to expend their excess energy through the movements. The exercise of creating new characters, dialogues and ideas for stories provide a creative outlet for their energies that will effectively occupy their time and prevent any potential for misbehavior as a result of ADHD. This allows them to focus and channel all of their creative energies into their chosen role (no matter what it may be). This type of structured group play promotes the development of executive thinking in that these permit the formation of collaborations between children to ensure that they know how to socialize, act in certain situations and determine reality from make-believe, as well as how to work as part of a team. Your intervention as a parent is needed to help them guide themselves into a story where the children cooperate with each other and listen to what each other wants.

Treasure hunts are a great way to integrate another form of activity such as nature walks, that can form part of a structured group play, and a great birthday party theme, provided that the necessary safety precautions have been taken care of. This does not involve a shovel however, so no digging will take place. One person is assigned to hide a treasure, while one person is assigned to find it later on. The child assigned to find the treasure stays outside a spot where they cannot see, while the one assigned to hide the treasure does their job. They can begin to find out what the treasure is by the other children yelling hot if the treasure is near, or cold if the treasure is far. This teaches the children how to develop patience and collaboration with their friends and also improves their ability to listen. Miming adds a new dimension as this allows your child and other children to improve their ability to read how people act even if they do not say anything.

Conclusion

Social skills are vital for every child, and though ADHD may present unique challenges in this area, these skills can be learned and enhanced. It requires the concerted effort of parents, teachers, and friends, regular practice, and constructive feedback. By employing the above strategies, you can support your ADHD child in developing essential social competencies, leading to stronger relationships and a more fulfilling life. These tactics help instill confidence, promote self-awareness, and provide practical ways for ADHD children to relate positively to their environment.

Remember, the road to improved social skills is a journey that will require patience, empathy, and consistent guidance. But with the right support, an ADHD child can flourish socially, building lasting friendships and thriving in their community.

3.6. Practices to Improve Listening Skills

This chapter will delve into the nuances of enhancing listening skills in your children, particularly those struggling with ADHD. The importance of fostering this skill cannot be overstated, especially considering that children, and more frequently those with ADHD, can often seem to "tune out" of a conversation or selectively hear what interests them. This can be highly noticeable in situations involving instructions they would rather not follow, such as requests to complete chores or stop playing video games. While it is quite normal for children to exhibit selective listening, it becomes a matter of concern when the behavior is persistent and consistent. This may indicate an underlying issue related to an inability to fully grasp or comprehend verbal communication. Whatever the underlying cause, the reassuring news is that listening skills are improvable. This section will guide you through understanding what listening entails and practical steps to enhance your child's listening ability.

Listening Skills Explained

Listening is often confused with hearing, yet there's a crucial distinction between the two. Hearing is a passive physiological process, whereas listening is an active process that involves comprehension and extracting meaning from what is heard. It enables children to hear, understand, and retell a story in their own words. Developing this skill is essential from a young age since effective listening forms the foundation for robust communication.

Why Poor Listening is Detrimental

Listening is vital for clear communication and significantly influences various aspects of a child's life. Here's how poor listening skills may negatively impact your child:

- Difficulty in Socialization: Lack of good listening skills can hinder your child's ability to interact with peers. They may become easily distracted during play, reducing the quality of interaction and hampering group activities. This may result in isolation and missed opportunities for social development.
- Challenges in Sound Awareness: Poor listening may also affect phonological awareness - recognizing, identifying, and working with different sounds. This can make it difficult for children to discern tones, emotions, and loudness, resulting in misunderstandings, struggles with following directions, and even behavioral issues.
- Academic Struggles: Since students rely on attentive listening throughout their school day, poor listening skills can impede learning in various subjects, particularly reading, grammar, and vocabulary. This could lead to more extensive academic challenges, affecting communication and making reading and comprehension more arduous.

The following chapters will outline specific strategies to address these challenges and promote better listening skills tailored to children with ADHD. Your child's ability to listen, understand, and communicate through targeted exercises and consistent practice can be significantly improved, laying the foundation for a successful and fulfilling life.

Listening Therapy

There are several methods by which a child with ADHD can be treated, aside from the use of psychopharmacologic methods, which is to say, the use of medication. While medication will be needed, it is not recommended however, to have the entire treatment regimen of your child dependent on medication due to the high potential for adverse effects the more the medication builds up with the body and surpasses the therapeutic levels in the body of your child. There are other means by which the child can be effectively treated for the symptoms of their ADHD, and this includes the use of other therapies. Other parts of this book have mentioned the use of structured group play as an effective means to lessen the symptoms of ADHD that manifest within the child. This context now deals with the use of listening therapy, part of which was glossed over as an activity suitable for you and your baby, now taken into the context of a child.

While the use of other psychoeducational therapies has been extolled in the treatment of the symptoms of ADHD, one of the more recommended therapeutic alternatives would be that of listening therapy, in this context, in reference to the use of music, though other sounds may be used as part of the treatment process provided that they are within the set recommendations for this form of therapy. The music experience of the child creates a subtle influence upon the perception of reward and consequences, the emotions of the child, their motivations and pleasures and the sensations that are derived from it, stress and the immune system of the child, socialization and their cognitive skills. Before you become skeptical about the effects, think back on your personal mood songs. Certainly, you do have songs that you use to study, songs that make you feel happy or sentimental, songs that boost your mood; it is in the same context that these songs are able to work for your child, and it gives their thought processes something else to fixate and potentially channel your child's energy through. This does not mean however, that you should impose your own musical taste onto your child at the moment, no. This means that you should take some time to help your child discover their own musical tastes and help them discover what kind of music they respond to. Sometimes you might be surprised by the results. After all, parents who have started reading and listening to their children from their infancy result in children who are more accustomed to certain sounds and are more sensitive to nuances in sound that show the emotion of a particular piece. It is expected then that children in whom this type of therapy has been started on are able to have a better grasp on emotions and how to better read a person, which also gives them an added boost on their socialization.

ADHD according to a study in 2021 Current Psychology, has its categorization as a neurodevelopmental disorder. This entails that children have certain difficulties in the development of their mental faculties which often place them two to three years behind other children. In the instance of ADHD however, their neurodevelopmental development is hindered in the sensorimotor, sensory integration or sensory processing problems. The children find difficulties in the detection, modulation and interpretation of stimuli compared to other children who were able to develop regularly. The child with ADHD would have difficulties then in the ability to listen to a person, or can be termed as selective listeners, although you will understand as a parent that they do not choose to listen selectively, but rather that this is an offshoot of the development of their brain. The child is unable to discriminate sounds on their own, and hence is unable to localize a sound as to whom the sound belongs to. Because of this, the child may simply opt to not react to the sound or over-react to the sound, which is not desirable on either end of the spectrum, hence the need to determine a range that is at least beneficial for the child in question.

There is an established link with the inability of the child to process sounds and the behavior that they manifest. Those who find difficulties with sound often exhibit depression, are unnaturally aggressive, may have oppositional -defiant disorder (ODD- where the child constantly opposes anything you might suggest they do), or conduct disorders – summarily, all of the behaviors characterized by their inability to adapt to a particular situation. Your child in this instance, is unable to understand what goes on around them clearly, and since they are unable to make sense of what is around them, they act out in the only way how, they misbehave in the hopes that someone will pay attention to them and help them understand what is going on. Ultimately, this all boils down to the ability of the child to understand the environment and the assurance that you as a parent would be able to assist them with their concern.

The development of a proper auditory system would be crucial to the improvement of the neurodevelopment of the child. You may want to ask your physician first if your child has a hearing problem, though presumably you have been informed by them beforehand if your child has exhibited such. That said, it is imperative then as part of this therapy to ensure that your child is exposed to as many sounds to stimulate their development, and one of the earlier recommended activities was to read to your child as early as possible. The various notes on a musical scale however, provide more variances as each note activates various parts of the brain and allow it to develop, which then makes the use of music as an effective means to develop the brain of the child over time. The brain itself is believed to be responsive to high frequency sounds, that is 3000 Hertz or more.

The effects of continued exposure to this type of frequency provide sufficient stimulation of the brain activity which increases the enthusiasm of the child with

ADHD, as well as promotes their overall emotional well-being, the development of their executive function and spatial reasoning. The latter might be a bit of a puzzle, but recall that in the previous paragraphs we have discussed the inability of the child with ADHD to localize sound. Their inability to localize sound may not necessarily stem from a defect in their hearing, but from the ability of their brain to process where the sound comes from. If for instance, your child becomes attuned to several types of sounds earlier on, they will be able to learn to localize sound, and if say, you call their name from across the room, they are more likely to be able to identify that it was you who called them, and their mind can form the association that the sound came from across the room, where you are. This leads to their development of not only their executive functions in their brain, but also their overall spatial awareness as they are able to determine the source of a sound that they have heard and understood to be familiar to them. If you try to make this an exercise, do not forget to reward your child. This is no small feat for them, given their high distractibility due to their ADHD.

In the selection of sounds for the performance of listening therapy, as parents, we have heard over time that the use of classical music (by composers such as Mozart, Beethoven, Bach and Chopin among others), leads to a higher cognitive development. There is actually some credence to this application as given their instrument of choice (the piano), leads to the production of high frequency sounds which lead to further brain stimulation and help fine tune a thought process that is otherwise chaotic – such as the thought processes of a child with ADHD. The simple chords that form the music are able to sufficiently stimulate a child and grab their attention without being too disruptive in other parts of their routine, so you may actually use this type of music as a means for your child to get ready for whatever activity is set out for them, as mentioned earlier in this book. The frequency of the sounds at this stage are purportedly able to improve the cognitive function of the child, and allows them to increase their attention span (a desirable effect in ADHD), organization and planning (if you integrate this form of music into their routine, they will be able to associate certain chords with certain cues in their routine), and abstract thinking (such as the expression of creative solutions on the part of the child). It is recommended that you choose the lighter and simpler forms of music for a more positive association (Bach's Minuet over Beethoven's Moonlight Sonata, for instance.) Conversely, music that produces low frequency sounds can also be used to help a child with ADHD calm down, as the low frequency of the sounds produced tend to soothe and relax and stimulate the motor function of the child, and hence allows them to feel more emotionally relaxed and safe. If you find this hard to believe, then recall instances where your child, as a baby, was able to calm down once you begin to hum and hold them close. They may be unable to understand what you hum, but they can feel it, and they associate it with relaxation, with the faintest memory that perhaps this is a sign that they are able to relax safely with their parent. If you find a hard time looking for sounds that carry a low frequency, you may opt to hold your child and hum songs instead. This gives you additional opportunities to not only bond with your child, but also to calm them down and assure them that you are always there for them.

There is a medium ground for the likes of listening therapy, as we have discussed the various benefits of low and high frequency forms of therapy upon the brain. Medium frequencies, such as our manner of speech are said to be conducive towards the development of communications skills in children with ADHD. Hence, it would be more than appropriate to integrate various forms of listening therapy for your child, with simplistic, rhythmic chords that foster the development of your child. You can understand now, why most children's songs are comprised of similar and simple chords, as these are the frequencies and patterns that their brains are more accustomed to, and which ground them in how they perceive their place in the world and how they are best able to react to it. Continued listening would at least ensure that they are grounded (the things that they hear), and orients them to a particular instance they are in at the moment. It is believed that the exposure of your child to various sounds as early as possible would help ease the regulation of their behavior later on. The use of listening therapy is believed to assist in the expansion of their attention span, improves their response to stimuli, and allows them better control over their impulsivity and hyperactivity through the improvement of the way their brain is able to process the sounds that they hear.

Summarily, the gist of the theory that underlies this therapy is that, if the child is able to better understand what they hear on a daily basis, the less likely they are to misbehave and act out in deference to their ADHD, hence the recommendation that you read and sing to your child as often as you can to ensure that your voice is the one that serves to orient your child to where they are at the moment. This lessens the opportunity for them to act out and provides more opportunities for them to behave and be rewarded by you for their good behavior.

White Noise and Memory Improvement

As parents, and more importantly as adults, we have developed an increased familiarity with the role of white noise and how it functions to help us sleep better. In this context however, the use of white noise does not involve its ability to make a person feel relaxed. What do I mean by this? Recall that your child with ADHD has their senses heightened to such a degree that they obtain stimuli from so many other sources in their environment that they do not know what to do, hence the manifestation of them acting out, because they find that they are unable to adapt to the stimuli that they sense. Where would white noise come in? White noise is defined as the summation of all noise comprised of various frequencies. We have touched upon the importance of various frequencies in the development of the ability of your child to retain and process information, and hence, the union of all of these frequencies in white noise would enable the stimulation of all the parts of the mind of the child. In line with this, studies have theorized that the application of white noise in the background while the child accomplishes task would provide sufficient amounts of stimulation needed to ensure that your child is able to accomplish the task at hand. The context of the study provided a situation wherein a child was subjected to an arithmetic test. Given what we know of math problems, you can expect that the child would either loathe the assignment or ignore it completely. It was shown that when white noise was played in the background as the children worked, the children were able to accomplish the task at hand, and were later documented to have improved verbal memory, inhibition control (a necessary action as children with ADHD are known for their inability to sense and react to danger), speech recognition (which is necessary to help them hone their ability to localize sounds and improve overall spatial awareness), and contribute overall to the improvement of the executive function of your child.

You might wonder then, between this form of therapy and the therapy provided for in the previous section, which of the two treatment methods are more appropriate for your child? Unfortunately, there is a relative lack of studies that can confirm which option is better for a child over the other, as both studies were more concerned with the development of the executive function of the child and how the use of various frequencies aid in its stimulation, rather than say, which treatment is more appropriate. Given that other forms of frequencies such as music, come in high, medium and low frequencies, exert various effects and white noise effectively combines all three frequencies into a unified version where the ear is able to perceive all three subliminally, the more logical assumption then follows that it would be best to utilize white noise in the background, particularly as your child works. That would be the most appropriate option, yet it would be advisable first to hold off on the purchase of white noise generators from your local shop. Why?

Admittedly, white noise, and any object that can generate them are well worth the investment placed into them, since they have the ability to stabilize the behavior of your child and ensure that they are able to have improvements in their cognitive and executive functions. This is not to completely discount the benefits of other forms of sound on their development, and hence, it would be necessary to ensure that there is application of both types of sound, wherein these past two sections were able to discuss areas wherein the application of various frequencies is best utilized in the development of the child. Low frequency sounds to let the child relax, high frequency sounds and white noises are best suited for situations where the child needs to accomplish a task, and medium frequency sounds are ideal for the day-to-day movements of the child such as the start of their routine. It was found at the conclusion of the study that white noise and white noise generators lead to improved cognitive development in a child, which make them the more viable option. When you do employ the use of white noise, it is not enough that you simply use the generator in the background. Remember that your child is highly distractible and you need to ensure that the noise is delivered in such a way that your child is unable to be distracted by other forms of stimulation. Noise-cancelling headphones or earphones are best suited for this to ensure that the music goes directly into the ear of your child.

The Use of Music Therapy in the Classroom

Parents and teachers would benefit from this section, particularly given that the continued use of white noise and music are shown to have a stabilizing effect upon the hyperactivity episodes and attention deficits of your child with ADHD. That aside, it would be necessary then to ensure that the appropriate methods are set up to ensure that the learning process is uninterrupted despite the use of an extraneous source of stimulation.

There are instances where the behavior of the child requires them to work in a structure environment on their own, and the use of music therapy as a form of stimulation of various parts of the brain leads to a decrease in the number of maladaptive behaviors in a child with ADHD. Subsequently, this means that the more your child listens to certain types of music, the more stable their emotional and cognitive thought processes are, which leads to an overall more improved outcome with regards to the use of music therapy in the child.

The type of music would have to be dependent upon the manifestations of ADHD in the child however, as some are just generally inattentive – where the main concern of the child is their inability to properly focus on the task at hand and is unable to follow a schedule set for themselves; some are too hyperactive – wherein the child's main concern is their restlessness; or a combination of both forms, which you are undoubtedly familiar with. It remains then, that the music therapy to be used in the classroom should be of a quality that ensures that the attention span of the student in question is maintained, that being in previous discussions, this quality was attributed to the use of high frequency sounds that are deemed to be more effective in the maintenance and the stabilization of the attention. The music chosen should not be considered as disruptive for the environment in the classroom, and if your child is homeschooled, the music you choose should not in any way serve to distract the child, otherwise you would find the use of this therapy to be otherwise ineffective.

It was stressed earlier that your child should have a role in the determination of the kind of music that they want, but if you find that they lean too much into a particular music type (such as Disney – there are only so many times you can hear a particular song), then you would be able to intervene through the use of a carefully curated musical playlist that you can use for the child. Children who are older and have developed their fine motor movements can at least benefit from the use of a musical instrument, which has the added benefit of giving them the ability to capture their attention and ensures that the child has more than enough opportunity to express their own creativity in such a way that their attention is sufficiently captured and thus, leads to a decrease in certain outbursts and episodes where maladaptive behavior of the child manifests. If your child does not favor the use of any musical instrument, that would be perfectly fine. What you can do then is to ensure that they do have music playing in their background as they perform classroom related activities as the use of music in their studies leads to the improvement of their overall cognitive development. The use of the musical instruments would have had an added benefit in that the continued use of fine motor movement would help regulate the movements of the child and prevent their tendencies to fall into accidents. For this form of therapy to be successful, it has to conform to the immediate needs of a student to ensure that they are at least cooperative and are given the attention that they perceive that they lack.

3.6.1. Characteristics of a Good Listener

Listening skills are vital for all children but can be particularly challenging for those with ADHD. As parents and caregivers, you can foster good listening habits by understanding and modeling these characteristics:

- Prepare Yourself for Listening: Children, particularly those with ADHD, might take more time to express themselves. Show patience and attentiveness as they navigate their thoughts.
- Be Attentive and Interested: Demonstrate a genuine interest in your child's words. Put away distractions and give your full attention, as

children with ADHD often need validation that they are being heard.

- Ask Engaging Questions: Asking questions during conversations or storytelling keeps your child engaged and helps reinforce comprehension.
- Allow Them to Speak Without Interruption: Even if they make mistakes or their narratives are disjointed, let them finish before offering guidance or correction.
- Notice Non-Verbal Communication: Pay attention to facial expressions, body language, and tone, as these might convey more than words, especially in children with ADHD.
- Encourage Open Communication: Facilitate an environment where your child feels comfortable sharing their thoughts and feelings. This will not only enhance their listening skills but also their expressive language abilities.

3.6.2. Active vs. Passive Listening

As mentioned earlier, your child's listening skills are key in their daily activities, especially at school. The two main listening skills are passive and active listening.

Active Listening

These listening skills involve giving all your attention and ensuring you fully understand the message. When listening actively, you're paying attention to every detail, including body language.

Importance of Active Listening for Children with ADHD:

Here are the benefits of being an active listener:
- More Independence: They become more capable of following instructions and completing tasks.
- Fewer Misunderstandings: Clear understanding leads to more appropriate responses and actions.
- Improved Resourcefulness: Helps in problem-solving and creativity.
- Enhanced Academic Performance: Contributes positively to their learning experiences.

Passive Listening

In contrast, passive listening lacks engagement and full understanding. It's merely hearing without processing the information. This type of listening might be more common in children with ADHD, but it's not conducive to their development:

- Lack of Engagement: This can lead to misunderstandings and missed opportunities for learning.
- Potential Social Challenges: This may affect their ability to interact with peers and build friendships.

3.6.3. Practical Strategies for Enhancing Listening Skills in Children with ADHD

- Use Visual Aids: Supporting verbal instructions with visuals can reinforce understanding.
- Break Instructions into Smaller Parts: Simplify complex instructions by breaking them down.
- Repeat and Reinforce: Repeat important information and ask your child to repeat it to ensure understanding.
- Provide Positive Reinforcement: Praise and reward good listening to reinforce this behavior.

These practical strategies, combined with an understanding of what good listening entails, can greatly assist you in fostering better listening skills in your child with ADHD. Remember, your patience and consistent effort can significantly affect your ability to communicate and interact with the world around you.

3.6.5. Your Role as a Parent in Developing Your Child's Listening Skills

As parents, nurturing your child's listening skills complements the efforts of teachers. This joint venture is vital, especially in children with ADHD, where listening might be more challenging. Remember, your reaction to their listening behavior will shape their habits, so focus on positive reinforcement rather than negative responses. For instance, you can praise your child when they follow instructions, signaling that they have listened well. Here are ways to foster this development:

- Be Patient: Developing listening skills is a gradual process. Patience and consistent practice are crucial.
- Make It Fun: Engage in enjoyable activities like listening to music, reading, or singing with your child.
- Reward Good Behavior: Acknowledge when your child pays attention, and reward them for it.

3.6.6. How to Nurture Good Listening Skills in Your Children

Creating an environment where listening is a pleasurable activity can have a significant impact on your child's development. Here are some interactive activities to help you nurture their listening skills:

- **Identify sounds:** Ask your kids to close their eyes and then play or make any sound and ask them to identify each sound.

- **Audio stories:** You can use many stories to improve your child's listening skills. Listen to these stories with your child and then ask them questions at the end. With this, they'll always want to pay attention so that they can correctly answer the questions you ask.

- **Add-on stories:** This is a good activity in which each participant adds to the story after five sentences.

- **Read stories to them:** You can read stories to your children, but ensure they pay attention to them. To make it interactive, you can ask for their thoughts or opinions about the story or even as them to predict the end of the story.

- **Games:** You can teach your children to focus on details and follow instructions. Use repetition games; for example, saying something and asking your child to repeat what you said. You can also play games like clapping a pattern, broken telephone, or any other copycat game.

One amazing thing is that these things are very easy to do, and they are all effective. You can use them to significantly improve your child's listening skills.

3.6.7. Recognizing Poor Listening Skills in Your Child

It is vital to identify if your child struggles with listening comprehension. Here's how you can detect signs of poor listening skills:

- Memory Lapses: Inability to remember recently communicated details.
- Difficulty with Rhymes and Songs: Struggling to learn or follow along with nursery rhymes.
- Comprehension Issues: Problems understanding mathematical words or following conversations.
- Reading and Spelling Challenges: Trouble spelling and reading may indicate a lack of understanding of sounds.
- Distraction: Frequent distraction, especially with background noise.

- Repetition Requests: Often asking for things to be repeated or difficulty following multi-step directions.

Children, whether or not they have ADHD, might experience listening problems. Some may outgrow them, while others, particularly children with ADHD, may need more support. Your active involvement in their auditory development is beneficial and essential as a parent.

3.7. How to Be a Positive Parent and Manage the ADHD Effects on Your Relationship (Marriage)

Parenting a child with ADHD can be challenging, and feeling overwhelmed and concerned about its effect on your marriage is natural. However, it is possible to nurture both your child and your relationship with understanding, teamwork, and compassion. Here is how:

Embracing Your Parenting Role:

- Believe in Yourself: Recognize that you are strong and capable. Affirm your abilities daily and maintain control over your emotions and reactions.
- Believe in Your Child: Focus on their strengths and potential. Encourage and support their growth and learning.
- Allow Flexibility: While rules are essential, flexibility is often required for children with ADHD, who might struggle with attention to detail.
- Seek Support: Join support groups or communities, and consult with therapists. Connecting with others in similar situations can provide invaluable encouragement.

Prioritizing Your Relationship:

ADHD can strain a relationship. However, with effort, communication, and empathy, you can overcome the challenges:

- Present a United Front: Agreement on parenting strategies eases the strain and instills confidence in your parenting roles.
- Spend Quality Time Together: Reconnect as partners, setting aside parental responsibilities to rediscover what brought you together.

- Compromise and Complement Each Other: Embrace differences by finding a middle ground and showing appreciation for each other's efforts.
- Consider Couples Therapy: Therapy isn't just for crises; it's a valuable tool for fostering communication and understanding how to navigate the complexities of parenting a child with ADHD.
- Exercise Patience: Diagnosis and treatment decisions might require time and collaboration. Support each other and act as a united team to determine your child's best approach.

Conclusion:

Parenting a child with ADHD can be a demanding experience, but it can also deepen the bonds within your family. Your child's diagnosis is not a limitation but an opportunity to learn resilience, empathy, and creativity in your parenting strategies. You can nurture a healthy family dynamic through collaboration and compassion, ensuring your child's well-being and the vitality of your relationship. By making these modifications, the revised section offers a more concise yet comprehensive guide that should resonate with parents dealing with ADHD. It avoids repetitive content and focuses on practical, compassionate strategies, leveraging my experience in this field.

3.8 Other Effective Management Options

In our earlier discussion on the pharmacological management of ADHD, we highlighted that while there's no cure for ADHD, various strategies can help manage the symptoms. Treatment for ADHD is multifaceted, encompassing medications, behavioral therapy, supplements, and dietary adjustments. In this chapter, we will explore in depth other supplementary methods to manage ADHD. Here's an overview of some therapeutic strategies:

- Psychotherapy: This approach enables children to articulate their feelings and discuss concerns. It involves counseling and Cognitive Behavioral Therapy (CBT), focusing on thoughts, feelings, and behavior. CBT builds self-esteem and addresses anxiety and depression, often linked with ADHD.
- Behavioral Therapy: Targeting negative behaviors for transformation into positive ones; this method involves collaboration between the child, parents, and counselor. Reward systems and parental training in behavior therapy complement medication to enhance self-esteem and self-control.

- Social Skills Training: If a child struggles with social interactions, this strategy teaches new, acceptable behaviors, such as patience, sharing, and handling teasing, aiding connections with others.
- Support Groups: A vital component in ADHD management, support groups offer community and shared experiences. Newly diagnosed patients, in particular, find solace and guidance here, ensuring they don't feel isolated.
- Use of Supplements: Some children may experience significant side effects from ADHD medications. In these cases, dietary supplements might be a helpful adjunct therapy but not a replacement. For example:
  - Zinc: Beneficial for brain health, found in foods like oysters, red meat, dairy products, whole grains, beans, and poultry, or as a tablet.
  - Omega 3 fatty acid: Essential for brain function, found in salmon, tuna, and mackerel, controlling neurotransmitter movement.
  - Iron: Used cautiously, iron supplements enhance neurotransmitter production, improving mood and emotion regulation.
  - Magnesium: Valuable only if deficient, found in dairy products, whole grains, beans, and leafy vegetables, to enhance mood and attention.
  - Melatonin: Though not directly impacting ADHD, it helps regulate sleep, a common ADHD side effect.
- Herbal Remedies: Ginkgo biloba, Korean ginseng, valerian root, and lemon balm; these natural supplements may alleviate hyperactivity and impulsiveness and enhance attention and sleep.

General Tips for ADHD Patients:
- Outdoor Time: Benefits children by enhancing concentration and mood.
- Yoga Classes: Boosts focus and attention, particularly those who enjoy the practice.
- Avoiding Allergens: Enhances attention and concentration.

In summary, managing ADHD requires a personalized and comprehensive approach, integrating various treatments tailored to the individual's needs. Collaboration between therapists, parents, and children is paramount for success. By exploring these options, families can create an environment that nurtures growth and development, allowing the child to thrive despite ADHD.

4 CONNECTING WITH YOUR CHILD

4.1 Effective Methods to Contrast Behavioral Challenges

Children with ADHD often face unique and complex behavioral challenges. Understanding these behaviors and developing strategies to cope with them can profoundly impact the child's well-being and the family's harmony.

Understanding the Behavioral Challenges

Children with ADHD are more likely to struggle with mental health issues such as anxiety, depression, self-injury, and substance abuse. These can manifest as aggressive behavior, defiance, emotional outbursts, and difficulty transitioning between activities.

- Aggressive Behavior and Defiance: Unlike their peers, children with ADHD may be prone to rebelliousness. They may resist instructions from parents or teachers, particularly during demanding tasks.

- Challenges with Transition and Boredom Tolerance: ADHD can lead to difficulty controlling impulses, tolerating dull situations, and shifting between different activities.

These issues may arise due to ADHD-related deficits, such as trouble controlling activity levels or paying attention. Knowledge and insight into these behaviors can lead to effective coping strategies.

Identifying Disorders Related to Defiance

Recognizing when defiance or disruptive behavior may signal an underlying disorder is essential. Frequent and severe instances of these behaviors may lead to the following diagnoses:

- Disruptive Mood Dysregulation Disorder (DMDD): DMDD describes continuous irritability and frequent, disproportionate temper or emotional outbursts. It often occurs alongside ADHD.

- Conduct Disorder (CD): This may include regular rule-breaking, aggressive, deceitful, or disruptive behavior. It is especially common in children with combined-type ADHD.

- Oppositional Defiance Disorder (ODD): If a child is consistently hostile, defiant, and uncooperative, they may be diagnosed with ODD. It is common in about 50% of children with combined-type ADHD and some with inattentive-type ADHD.

Strategies to Address Behavioral Challenges

Parents of children with ADHD are often beset with the maladaptive behaviors of their children with ADHD. The natural tendency for both parents and teachers is to scold the child. This action would be an exercise in futility as the child is unable to control the impulsiveness in their behavior as this is fully outside of their control. Hence, there is the need to establish a collaborative effort with teachers and counselors to determine what are the most effective strategies to address the challenges in the behavior of the children.

Professional guidance is one of the tools that are considered as the first-line behavioral intervention and that is deemed to be a necessity in schools that have large populations of children with ADHD. Parents may find it odd that this section would focus more on behavioral intervention given that it was stated earlier that the child would not have adequate control of their impulses. Studies have shown that the implementation of first-line behavioral interventions would be a more cost-effective measure for the parents as this is believed to reduce the need for additional ADHD medication on the part of the child to help control their behavior.

This counters the tendency where the child is medicated in sufficient quantities and dosages to ensure that they are more manageable in school times. However, with recent effects of medications taken into account on the development of the child, it becomes necessary then to ensure that the children are treated with interventions that are not solely reliant on the use of medication. The theory behind this type of parenting strategy lies on the knowledge that the children do not know that what they manifest is wrong. What they know is that their mind tells them that they must do this, and as such, they feel compelled to act in a particular manner.

One of the necessary steps then, aside from the development of a strong, collaborative effort between you as a parent and the teacher of the child, is the use of behavioral consultations. The use of behavioral consultations would have to vary upon the severity of the symptoms that manifest in the child, with low-intensity behavioral treatments utilized for milder cases of ADHD, while high-intensity behavioral treatments are utilized for more severe cases of ADHD. Regardless of the intensity however, the continued use of this type of intervention involves the reduction in the need for medication during times when the child is at school, a reduction for medications at home, and if done in increased frequencies, the child would be able to eliminate the need for medication altogether, which makes this a more cost effective mechanism, although it is observed that the costs of medication are supplanted by the use of behavioral consultations, although this would be up to you as a parent to decide as you know your child best.

There are alternatives that have been found in other studies, such as the use of the School-Wide Positive Behavioral Interventions and Supports (SWPBIS) which were found to be just as effective as the use of Behavioral Consultations in the reduction of the need for medication in children with ADHD. Under this intervention, it is believed that the socialization aspect of the child is taken into consideration, given that the application of this intervention is used throughout the entire school. Behavioral consultations by comparison are more engaged with the treatment of the symptoms, as it is centered on the knowledge that the child needs to be informed that their behavior is unacceptable and provides steps on what the child can do. Under the SWPBIS however, the children are taught more on the skills that they would need to help overcome their more impulsive tendencies with occasional supplementation of their medication to ensure that their behaviors exhibited are more manageable.

Under the auspices of this type of intervention, it requires the involvement of the school to create an environment that is accommodative of the needs of the child with ADHD. Critical factors under this include the capabilities of the school faculty, and the production of an environment where there is no tolerance for behaviors that can adversely affect the student such as bullying, aggression, truancy, and vandalism. The school environment then, must be one that prevents the distraction of the student and be more conducive to let the student learn, outside of the strategies that have been earlier outlined in this book.

Due to the nature of this type of intervention, it is noted that other students would benefit from this type of behavioral intervention, not only those students who have ADHD. There are several levels of interventions in accordance with the behaviors manifested by the student, just as the behavioral consultations have their own respective levels that cater to how irascible the student may be. That said, where the consultations are more passive in their approach, the use of the SWPBIS ensures that the whole school is involved to ensure that there is a safe environment for the children with ADHD, and other behavioral concerns.

Parents and caregivers must be equipped with tools to manage these behaviors. However, it must be understood that some tools may be out of reach for the parents, hence the need to establish resourcefulness in how the parent is able to help their child. Here are some strategies that may help you:

- Positive Reinforcement: Reward and acknowledge good behavior. It encourages repetition and helps build self-esteem. This does bear repetitions, but your child does act the way they do because they feel that there is a need that you have to address. They require lots of love and attention and be sure to amply reward them with your presence. Teachers would have to have the same approach as well, as your children would also come to expect the same level of warmth from you, as they would from their parents.

- Consistent Discipline: Maintain clear and consistent rules to provide a structured environment for the child. One of the main concerns is how you implement the importance of consequences upon a child so they will know their limits. Discipline in this instance does not require that you be harsh as a parent, but you do have to let them know their limits on their misbehavior that they would be able to better control themselves.

- Seek Professional Guidance: Engaging a mental health professional specializing in ADHD can provide tailored strategies and support. This was mentioned earlier at the start of this section and is echoed throughout the book.

- Educate and Collaborate: Collaborate with teachers and school staff to understand your child's needs and create an educational plan that accommodates their ADHD. Educational plans aside, you would also have to ensure that the routine you have at home adheres closely enough to that of the school to ensure that you are consistent in your applications.

- Build Emotional Resilience: Teach your child coping skills and emotional regulation techniques to help them handle their emotions constructively.

Understanding ADHD-related behavioral challenges and taking proactive measures can foster a more supportive environment for children and their families. It empowers parents and caregivers to connect with their children and helps the child navigate daily life with confidence and grace.

4.1.1. Parent Training Strategy

Parenting a child with ADHD can be a unique and complex challenge. However, it can be made manageable with the right training and strategies. Below are some revised details about two effective approaches that parents may find valuable:

Parent-Child Interaction Therapy (PCIT)

This hands-on approach encourages parents to interact with their children while receiving guidance from a therapist. Through life coaching, parents will learn to:

- Enhance and foster a positive relationship with their child
- Recognize and reinforce their child's positive behaviors
- Establish effective consequences for aggressive or disruptive behavior
- Ignore or manage minor misbehaviors, focusing on positive reinforcement

Parent Management Training (PMT)

This training method provides skills to parents in the absence of the child. It offers the same benefits as PCIT, with a more parent-focused approach. Key areas of training include:

- Reducing stress through understanding ADHD and its challenges
- Implementing strategies to reduce aggression and disobedience
- Learning how to pay attention to and thus encourage positive behaviors

Both PCIT and PMT effectively improve the child-parent relationship and address behavioral challenges faced by children with ADHD.

4.2 Identifying Your Discipline Philosophy

There are different discipline philosophies, and you must learn which will work best for your child with ADHD. This chapter focuses on the different discipline philosophies and provides an effective strategy for your child with ADHD. One of the toughest and most challenging parts of parenthood is discipline. This can discourage, humble, or frustrate you. Whenever you face these challenges, you might feel nostalgic about when they were just babies and how easy it was to handle them. All you need is to find an ideal philosophy matching your style. However, you need to know how and when to use these philosophies.

Interestingly, you can select more than one discipline philosophy and leave the rest. What matters most is using the right philosophy for your child with ADHD. As you read the philosophies below, I strongly advise you to pay attention to your feelings while reading each style.

4.2.1. How do the discipline theories differ?

There is so much advice from different experts; when you hear these, it will only confuse and frustrate you. For example, while one expert says that time-outs will only last a minute, another says your child will decide how long a time-out will last. Also, in some books, you'll be advised not to use words like "don't" and "no," other books will outrightly ask you to use these words when correcting your child. All of these only cause more confusion. The truth is that even though these people are experts, and the recommendations will work in some situations, the ultimate expert when determining what will work for your child is you. Yes, you are the only true expert determining the type of discipline to use on your child. Professional advice is important and helpful, but I always advise parents to merge this with their ideals and intuition.

4.2.2. The Discipline Philosophies

Boundary-based discipline

Sometimes, a child will only feel safe when there's a boundary. They'll continue to try different things until they can identify where such boundaries exist. A child will want to know what will happen if they throw the key away or use an object to make a noise. Most children will want to test limits to see their parent's reactions. If you're patient, you don't have to wait for them to be inquisitive and decide to push these boundaries. Effective communication is essential here. It is crucial to convey limits to your children as parents. Also, please have your child put toys away when they're done with them. You can also attach a consequence for not doing these things correctly, but the consequence should be logical enough. It's always best to utilize natural consequences. For example, leaving your child to experience the consequence of forgetting their lunch box at home. Rather than rush to get it to them, you can decide to delay a little.

Gentle Discipline

Children can't learn when they are in tears or screaming. There's so much for you and your child to benefit from when you use daily preventive strategies. This has a higher tendency to reduce misbehavior. You can create routines that will make your child feel grounded. Give them choices and make them feel in control. Whenever there's a transition, always give them prior notice. For example, when they're playing in the garden, and you're due to go out, you can give them ten minutes' notice before you leave rather than asking them to leave on the spot. Ensure that your request to them is always positive. Also, try to be strategic with your response to them. For example, when your child asks to go out to play but is yet to do homework, you might be tempted to say NO. However, the best thing is to say, "You can go out after completing your homework." A child's misbehavior may sometimes result from hunger, boredom, or tiredness. You need to pay attention to these because once the initial issue has been resolved, they won't misbehave anymore.

Positive Discipline

One way to ensure that your child behaves well all the time is by ensuring that they have a sense of belonging and feel encouraged. Children will always misbehave whenever they feel discouraged. Always communicate with your child, and don't be quick to judge them when they misbehave. Try to find out the cause of their misbehavior. For example, if your child refuses to wash the dishes, rather than shout at them, you can try to find out why. Shouting at children will only instill fear. But when you sit your kids down to reason with them, it gives them a sense of belonging. Once you have identified their reason for not doing something, you can encourage them or find a solution to help them work better. The whole idea about positive discipline is utilizing misbehavior and turning it into a learning opportunity for your child.

Emotion-coaching

Helping children understand their feelings will help them make better decisions. Therefore, parents need to teach their kids how to understand their emotions. Doing this will also help you connect with your child. The first thing you should do is identify your standards and know what you can and won't accept. From there, you can communicate these things with your child and ensure that you let them understand some of the feelings they are likely to experience. Always try to put yourself in their shoes and see what they a feeling. That way, you'll be able to understand why they are misbehaving. This will also help you know how to communicate your feelings with them.

Behavior modification

You can alter good and bad behaviors. All you have to do is utilize positive reinforcement to increase good behaviors and negative reinforcement to cause a decline in bad behaviors. You might want to think this approach is similar to the boundary-based discipline philosophy. However, the difference is that behavior modification places more emphasis on rewards and warnings. With warnings, you can help your child stop misbehaving and teach them to take responsibility for their actions. Sometimes, you might need to give these warnings a couple of times until you achieve your goal. In cases where the offense is serious, you can devise a consequence that will help them realize they are misbehaving. With rewards, you can motivate your child. It doesn't have to be extravagant; simple parental praise can do the job. As parents, always try to reward your child when they behave well. These are the different discipline philosophies, and they overlap each other. Now that you know these philosophies, we can move on to strategies to help you.

4.2.3. Discipline Strategies for an ADHD Child

Disciplining a child with ADHD can be arduous, and you might need different approaches to achieve this. You can easily help your child manage their behavior with a few parenting strategies. Here are some discipline strategies I recommend:

- **Provide positive attention:** It is exhausting to parent a kid with ADHD. Your child will always have an intense urge to keep talking. Additionally, their energy levels are high and may be worn out in the long term. The best gift you can give your kid is your attention. No matter how busy your schedule will ever get, always try to devote time to your children, even if it's just 15 minutes.

- **Praise their efforts:** Do not hesitate to congratulate your child whenever you observe them doing something nice. Praise will motivate them. Therefore, try to praise them frequently. When praising your kids, ensure it is as specific as possible.

- **Give effective instructions:** For a child with a short attention span, you'll need to be careful when giving them instructions. Also, they may require further assistance in following instructions. Sometimes, your child may not hear what is said the first time and may need you to repeat yourself. Before instructing your child, always try to get their full attention. You can eliminate every form of distraction, such as turning off the television and maintaining eye contact with them.

- **Ignore mild misbehaviors:** Attention-seeking behavior is very common in ADHD children. That is why you must always give them all the attention they want. While doing this, you are likely to observe some mild misbehaviors. You don't have to always point out these misbehaviors. Sometimes they are to get your attention, and when you ignore them for a while, they will stop.

- **Use time-out when necessary:** This is an effective way to help your ADHD child calm their brain and body. Time-out doesn't mean harsh punishment, but it's a useful life skill in many situations. Let your child know the importance of going to a quiet place and staying quiet for a period, especially when frustrated or overstimulated. When doing this, try to ensure they don't get the idea that you're punishing them for misbehaving. With time, your child will learn to go to quiet places when hyperactive.

- **Use natural consequences:** Disciplining a child with ADHD requires wise actions. When doing this, always ensure your child does not start thinking they don't get anything right. Sometimes, when you let some behaviors slide, you are helping yourself and your child. In many cases, natural consequences teach kids not to repeat some things they did in the past. You don't have to force a child to eat breakfast before school. Allow their wish to prevail, and watch the results. In this case, hunger is the natural consequence.

- **Work with their teacher:** Working with your child's teacher will help increase their school's success. Sometimes a child with ADHD will require specific school work modifications, such as extended test times. You might also need to include behavioral modifications sometimes. When doing this, it is advisable to ensure that it's continuous both at home and in school.

- **Reward systems:** This is an effective way to make your child maintain focus on what they do. However, using the conventional reward system in which a child must wait long to get can only bore a child with ADHD. Sometimes you might need to use a token-based system in which your child will earn throughout the day. Rewards will come in handy in teaching your child to do things right and help them stay motivated and focused.

4.3 Mastering Effective Communication Methods

One of the challenges with parenting a child with ADHD is communication. Upon interacting with different parents with an ADHD child, I've come to realize that most of these parents sometimes find it hard to communicate with their children. Sometimes, they do not know the best way to make their children understand simple things, which can be frustrating. Sometimes, they do not know how to get their children to follow directions, slow down, or pay attention to important things. The communication problem becomes worse if the parent has ADHD. As a parent, one thing you should understand is that the mind of a child with ADHD is always busy. It's safe to imagine their brain as a very busy city with different information, sensory input, impulses, directions, and many other distractions. However, in this city of theirs, there are no traffic lights, which only causes chaos and confusion. Maintaining effective communication with your child is very important. It is what will determine if your directions are clear enough. Also, when communicating with your child, always give them choices and break tasks into smaller units. Rather than making statements, you can decide to ask questions. Doing this will force your child to think of possible alternatives. You need to understand that for a child with ADHD, you'll require more than just talking to communicate with them. These children are special; if you are not careful, you'll only talk until your face turns blue, and your child still doesn't understand what you're trying to say.

Most parents don't usually know how to handle temper tantrums which are likely to occur frequently in a child with ADHD, especially if they are frustrated or having an emotional outburst. It is beneficial for parents to view these temper outbursts as a chance to demonstrate their honesty. To succeed, you must tell your child their tantrums will not harm you. Staying cool is one of the most effective methods to soothe a child with regular tantrums. You should notice emotional outbursts or meltdowns and attempt to remain calm and observe the situation. The best way to demonstrate to your child that you are the adult in their life and that you have everything under control is to provide stability confidently.

Your child needs to see you as an emotionally strong person who can handle their tantrums, no matter how severe they may be. Your child might already be used to seeing you get upset whenever they show these tantrums. Therefore, trying something new will make them stop and think. Imagine if, rather than raising your voice or losing it, you sit down, drink water or do something different to stay calm. This will take your child by surprise, and they'll also be forced to calm down. Once calm, you can invite them to your space and talk to them. When you do this, you are helping your child understand that you are emotionally strong, and soon, you'll become their hero. Whether your child has ADHD or not, communicating with them is very important. For children with ADHD or any other attention issue, communication can be hard, leading to misunderstandings in different ways. Here are strategies that you can use to strengthen communication with your child:

- **Explain your expectations:** Attempt to explain things to your child as plainly as possible. This ensures they have a clear idea of what is expected of them and what should be avoided. Teaching youngsters what is expected of them and what they may anticipate in return will positively affect their behavior. You can also support this strategy by using rewards for positive behaviors.

- **Remain calm and talk softly:** Feeling agitated or wanting to raise your voice is normal. However, always remember that this will only stimulate your child. Always try to stay calm and speak quietly whenever your child is upset. You can also step away whenever they start to throw tantrums. I recommend anything quiet activity during this time rather than raising your voice at them.

- **Visual aids:** Visual aids have proven effective for kids with ADHD, and you might want to consider using them. You can use these visual aids to communicate effectively with your kids. Rather than telling them what to do, you can make representations of these things on posters and show them to your child.

- **Choices:** Whenever a child notices that you are talking at them and not to them, they are likely to tune you out. However, giving them choices will make it a lot easier for them to pay attention to what you're saying. They will analyze both options and see which suits them more. For example, when you ask your child to wear their pajamas, they will likely ignore you. However, when you say, "Would you like to wear the blue pajamas or the yellow ones?" your child will think and choose one.

- **Create communication strategies:** Communicating with a child with ADHD will require you to apply creative measures. It's not an easy journey, so you'll need a very high level of patience. Be open to trying different communication strategies until you have found one that works.

- **Give simple and short directions:** Children become overwhelmed easily, even more, when they have ADHD. Always give step-by-step instructions whenever you want a child with ADHD to perform a task. However, you'll need to be careful when giving these instructions. Avoid giving all the steps at once because they will likely forget everything. Please give them a few instructions first and then wait for them to complete them before proceeding to the next steps.

- **Recognize when your child is paying attention or simply hearing you:** You cannot always expect them to maintain eye contact with you, and this doesn't mean they are not listening to you. You'll be surprised to know they are listening even though they are playing with another object. Whenever you talk to your child, always pay attention to their every move, and find cues that suggest whether they are listening.

4.4 A peaceful connection

It is not enough to say you love and care for your child. Everybody can talk, but what are you doing to show that you love and care for them? How you care for a child with ADHD differs from how you care for others. It is easy to have everything planned out in your head, but are you caring and connecting with your child correctly? Loving and connecting with children with ADHD can seem impossible due to the effects of the disorder, but the fact remains that all children deserve love and affection. The process might seem impossible, but it's achievable. Below are some tips to help you connect with your child with ADHD.

- **Be ready to put in the work:** To make anything work, you must be ready to put your strength and energy into it. You must be ready to leave your comfort zone and shake yourself up a little. You will often feel like giving up or just throwing in the towel but remember that you have a child that needs your care and support.

- **Create a comfortable atmosphere for the child:** Things will flow naturally when the environment is comfortable and serene for both the child and the parent. When a child feels comfortable in an environment, it is easy for them to open up about what they are going through.

- **Build trust with your child:** A popular adage says trust is earned and not demanded. As a parent, it is easy to demand trust because you feel it is your right instead of forcing trust on the child. Trust could mean delivering your promise to them; if you know you would not be able to keep to your promise, do not make them. Trust could also mean showing up no matter what. If you are to pick up your child from school at the said time, DO IT. If you know you want to attend a baseball game they are playing, SHOW UP. This helps build and foster trust.

- **Do not hold hurt against them:** For children with ADHD, it is normal for them to forget your instructions because they find it hard to concentrate. It would help if you remembered that they were not doing it intentionally. Sometimes you may become angry at them for not completing tasks or meeting deadlines, but you must always let go. Do not hold these issues against them, or it will affect your relationship.

- **Create healthy communication:** Pay attention to your children and their unvoiced desires and feelings. Instead of ignoring people, please pay attention to them and speak to them freely about subjects you usually wouldn't. You lose out on learning and teaching by rejecting your child as soon as they talk to you. Then, they understand that you aren't attentive, which makes communication pointless.

- **Use the right disciplinary measures:** You may resort to spanking to discipline your child with a long-term solution. Spanking has the benefit of providing parents with short-term compliance. But this approach is ineffective in teaching children about right and wrong. Instead, it simply encourages the child to dread repercussions outside of the situation. Then they fear being caught, which motivates them to avoid it. Some statistics show that spanked children are prone to fighting and may become bullies. Other ways to correct your child include:

  - **Make consequences clear:** Reassure your child that their actions will result in consequences, including taking away privileges or restricting their activities. However, it would help if you didn't remove things your child needs.

  - **Give them a chance to explain:** Listen to your child and pay close attention to what they say. You will be surprised at the things you will learn and be able to solve. Talk to your child rather than lashing out every time.

  - **You don't have to respond to everything:** Responding to every mistake your child makes will end up frustrating you and your child because they will likely feel that they never get everything right. You should overlook many things for your mental health; don't get me wrong, your child needs to be corrected, but when you can turn a blind eye to a mistake, you should do it.

- **Set rules:** It is very important for your children to know what is expected of them. For children with ADHD, they might need constant reminders about what is expected of them. Rather than being quick to spank your child, take out time to explain what you need them to do.

Parenting a child with ADHD might be different from what we all know. Home customs and traditions could be difficult to teach to your child. Creating family traditions could be impossible, depending on how severe the effects of ADHD are. Although the symptoms of ADHD are very frustrating to deal with as a parent, always try and reaffirm that your child who is ignoring, annoying, or embarrassing you is not doing so intentionally. Your child wants to make you happy, obey instructions, and be organized, but they can't help themselves. You must learn to manage your child's behavior and seek treatments and medications. You must understand that it's not easy for your child, just as it is for you. You and your child can have an easier journey with care, love, and unwavering support.

4.5 Advanced Strategies for Parenting an ADHD Child

The strategies for parenting ADHD children presented in the past chapters come from my experience and the studies of other experts in these books:
Behavioral Therapy and Positive Reinforcement:
- Prominent in books like "Parenting Children with ADHD" by Vincent J. Monastra.
- Emphasizes positive reinforcement, consistency in rules, and clear communication.

Mindfulness and Connection:
- As advocated by Dr. Mark Bertin in "Mindful Parenting for ADHD."
- Focuses on mindfulness practices, understanding child's perspective, and empathy.

Understanding the ADHD Brain:
- Dr. Daniel Amen's "Healing ADD" offers insights into different types of ADHD and personalized approaches.
- Uses brain scans to understand ADHD and offers tailored strategies including diet, supplements, and lifestyle changes.

Structured Environment and Routine:
- Books like "Taking Charge of ADHD" by Russell A. Barkley emphasize creating a structured environment.
- Daily routines, visual schedules, and clear expectations are key components.

Collaborative and Problem-Solving Approach:
- Ross Greene's "The Explosive Child" encourages collaborative problem solving.

- Working with the child to understand their difficulties and jointly finding solutions.

Integrative Treatment Approach:
- In "The ADD & ADHD Answer Book" by Susan Ashley, there's an emphasis on combining medical treatment with behavioral strategies.
- Customized strategies include therapy, medication, school interventions, and family support.

Emphasizing Strengths and Interests:
- As seen in "Superparenting for ADD" by Edward M. Hallowell and Peter S. Jensen.
- Focuses on building on the child's strengths and passions, rather than just addressing weaknesses.

Technology and Innovative Tools:
- Some modern guides include the use of apps, games, and technological aids in therapy and learning.
- Encourages the use of interactive learning platforms and digital tracking of progress.

Nutrition and Holistic Health:
- Books like "The ADD Nutrition Solution" by Marcia Zimmerman emphasize dietary changes.
- Focuses on understanding how food allergies, intolerances, and nutritional deficiencies can affect behavior.

Family Dynamics and Sibling Relationships:
- "ADHD: What Every Parent Needs to Know" by Michael I. Reiff delves into family relationships.
- Addresses how ADHD affects siblings and the family as a whole, offering strategies for harmony.

These strategies present a multifaceted approach to parenting children with ADHD. Different authors and experts bring their perspectives and research, offering a rich array of tools and approaches that can be tailored to individual families' needs and situations. The focus ranges from scientific and medical insights to more empathetic and intuitive approaches, providing a comprehensive view of ADHD parenting strategies. Below, I present to you some of my more sophisticated strategies that more heavily involve play and the child's emotional aspect. I especially recommend these to parents who are already well-versed in the subject.

Structured Game Time
- Puzzle Solving: Engage your child in puzzles that require focus and attention. It helps in developing concentration.
- Outdoor Adventure Games: Activities like scavenger hunts can make use of a child's energy and creativity. Include clues that challenge their thinking and reward their efforts.

Tailored Reward System

- Token Economy: Create a system where your child can earn tokens for positive behavior. These can be exchanged for desired rewards.
- Visual Progress Charts: Use charts to track behavior or academic progress, with rewards for reaching specific milestones.

Technology-Driven Learning Tools

- Educational Apps: Apps like "Epic!" or "DragonBox" provide interactive learning in math and reading tailored to the child's level.
- Virtual Reality (VR) Games: Some VR games are designed for therapeutic purposes, helping children with ADHD to improve their focus and impulse control.

Therapeutic Playtime

- Sensory Bins: Fill containers with sand, rice, or water beads and hide objects inside. This activity encourages focus and tactile exploration.
- Art Therapy: Encourage expression through painting, sculpting, or drawing. Art activities can provide a calming and focused experience.

Involvement in Sports and Hobbies

- Martial Arts: Disciplines like Karate or Taekwondo teach self-control, patience, and focus.
- Musical Instruments: Learning an instrument requires concentration and regular practice, providing a productive outlet for energy.

Interactive Storytelling and Role-Playing

- Create Your Story: Write a story together, taking turns adding sentences or paragraphs. Make it as wild or fantastical as you like!
- Role-Playing Games: Engage in role-playing games that require cooperation, negotiation, and creative thinking.

Mindfulness and Relaxation Practices

- Children's Yoga: Guided yoga sessions designed for children can enhance self-awareness and control.
- Breathing Exercises with Visuals: Use a pinwheel or bubbles to practice deep, calming breaths.

Diet and Nutrition Activities

- Cooking Together: Teach the value of nutrition by cooking healthy meals together. Make it fun by trying new recipes.
- Nutrition Tracking: Create a weekly chart tracking different vitamins and nutrients, and how they contribute to overall health.

Family Projects and Team Building

- Family Garden: Planting and caring for a garden encourages responsibility and focus.

- Weekly Challenges: Create weekly family challenges that promote teamwork and strategy.

Educational Field Trips and Exploration

- Nature Trails: Exploring nature trails with educational stops can be both engaging and instructive.
- Museum Visits with Activities: Plan visits to museums that align with school subjects and include interactive tasks related to exhibits.
- Conclusion

These advanced strategies are designed to provide practical, hands-on solutions that engage children with ADHD in creative and thoughtful ways. From game-driven learning to family-centered activities, these ideas strive to tap into the child's interests, energy, and capabilities. The emphasis is on making the learning process fun, interactive, and rewarding, building a more nuanced approach that goes beyond routine management. By crafting these activities with your child's unique needs in mind, you can create a supportive and stimulating environment that nurtures their growth and development.

5 CONCLUSION

ADHD is a completely manageable disorder that is common in children and adults. Managing a child with ADHD can be arduous; if care is not taken, parents might lose their temper or ignore the child's condition, which can even make matters worse. In most cases, ADHD usually occurs alongside other issues like anxiety and depression, all completely manageable. Parenting children with ADHD is not as easy as it may sound, especially for parents with the condition. The first thing you should do as a parent is to understand everything about the condition. Fortunately, this book has covered all the key aspects of ADHD and even more. With this, you have all the information you need; the only thing left is to start applying this information in managing your child's condition. In the first part of this book, I covered the medical aspects of ADHD; I talked about ADHD and the treatment used, particularly drug therapy. There are many drug treatment options for children with ADHD, including stimulants and non-stimulants. However, this information is not provided so that you become your child's prescriber. Always consult a physician before giving your child any medication.

In the second part of the book, I provided information that can further help you understand your child's condition. When you understand the condition, you'll be able to come up with effective strategies to handle it. I also provided tips to help you navigate through tantrums. The third part of the book centered on managing your child's condition with methods other than the use of drugs, while the fourth chapter focused on providing ways to help parents connect with their children.

With all this, you can comfortably manage your child's ADHD and prevent it from affecting their day-to-day activities. Raising a child with ADHD comes with its own set of unique difficulties. However, as a parent of a child with ADHD, you should never forget that there are no shortcuts to learning. This is because ADHD expresses itself with different symptoms and degrees of severity. With a tailor-made or person-centered approach, your child will enjoy great benefits. Poor impulse control leading to inappropriate and challenging behaviors is a common symptom of ADHD. However, the first step for every parent is to accept their child's condition and come to terms with the fact that ADHD is nothing more than a functional difference in their child's brain.

Also, having a child with ADHD doesn't mean that the child will not be able to distinguish right from wrong. There are so many ways to support and help an ADHD child to develop positive behavior. Another important thing is for caregivers and parents to find ways to interact with ADHD children. This includes gestures, physical environment, emotional language, and speech. Using structured and supportive approaches can significantly help reduce challenging behaviors and help the child excel. There are so many ongoing studies into ADHD. New and effective ways of living with the condition are tested regularly, including sociological, psychological, and medical. Unlike a few decades ago, ADHD is more socially accepted, which is great for managing the condition. This also helps support parents and caregivers of children with ADHD. Interacting with ADHD children requires much care. In general, these children are usually first diagnosed with ADHD when they are 7 years old, which is very young. Maintaining a conversation with a normal 7-year-old child can be difficult and more difficult with an ADHD child. However, despite these difficulties, it is important to speak to the child regularly because this can benefit both the parent and the child. Always try to use age-appropriate language when conversing. Remember that you do not want to give unnecessary details before achieving your goal. Also, with more conversations about ADHD, the child's curiosity about their condition increases. With that in mind, here are statements that can help you start a conversation with an ADHD child:

- **ADHD is not a flaw**: Help the child understand that their condition is not bad, neither a flaw nor a weakness. It doesn't make other kids better than they are, and it is like every other condition that, when supported correctly, won't affect the person's life negatively.

- **ADHD does not affect intelligence**: An ADHD child can be as smart as every other child. When you talk to your kids, always try to remind them that so many great thinkers had ADHD right from when they were kids. Examples include Thomas Edison and Albert Einstein.

- **You can succeed in life, even with ADHD**: You can provide your child with positive role models, particularly those who have succeeded. So many celebrities have had to deal with ADHD, including Solange Knowles

96

and Will Smith. Allow your child to admire these people and let them be their motivation. Even though having a child with ADHD requires much thinking and planning, the whole process becomes fulfilling and pleasurable, especially when you obtain the desired results.

6 REFERENCES

- American Psychiatric Association. (2013). Diagnostic and statistical manual of mental disorders (5th ed.). Arlington, VA: Author.
- Siegel, D. J., & Bryson, T. P. (2016). No-drama discipline: the whole-brain way to calm the chaos and nurture your child's developing mind. Trade Paperback Edition. New York: Bantam Books.
- Siegel, D. J., & Bryson, P. H. D. T. P. (2012). The whole-brain child. Random House.
- Ian P Stolerman (2010), Encyclopedia of Psychopharmacology, Springer
- www.additudemag.com/what-is-adhd-symptoms-causes-treatments/
- Mengühan Araz Altay, Işık Görker, Begüm Demirci Şipka, Leyla Bozatlı, Tuğçe Ataş (2020), Attention Deficit Hyperactivity Disorder and Psychiatric Comorbidities, Euras J Fam Med
- www.blogarama.com/health-and-fitness-blogs/1295402-healthinfi-secure-health-blog/23895434-about-addadhd
- Harris R. Lieberman (2007) Cognitive methods for assessing mental energy, Nutritional Neuroscience, 10:5-6, 229-242, DOI: 10.1080/10284150701722273
- Balbinot P, Testino G (2020) The Introduction of Self-Help Group Facilitator in an Alcohol Unit: Preliminary Results. Int Arch Subst Abuse Rehabil 2:008. doi.org/10.23937/2690-263X/1710008
- www.ninds.nih.gov/disorders/patient-caregiver-education/fact-sheets/tourette-syndrome-fact-sheet
- www.churchillstl.org/learning-disability-resources/adhd/
- www.fiercebiotech.com/biotech/head-to-head-study-demonstrates-focalin-r-xr-offers-faster-and-better-symptom-control-than
- EAPC Abstracts. Palliative Medicine. 2019;33(1):118-589. doi:10.1177/0269216319844405

7 WORKBOOK FOR PARENTS

7.1 Personal Reflections

Understanding your unique experience with ADHD is crucial. Reflect on the following questions and jot down your thoughts. There is no right or wrong answer here – this is about your experience.

- How has ADHD affected your daily life or the life of your child?
- What strategies have you found most successful in managing ADHD symptoms?
- Are there any specific challenges that you feel need more attention or support?

Answers:

7.2 Building a Personalized Strategy

1. Identifying Strengths and Challenges

A. Strengths: List three strengths you or your ADHD-affected child possesses. Think about talents, abilities, or traits that stand out.

B. Challenges: List three challenges faced due to ADHD. Consider daily routines, social interactions, or learning environments.

C. Strategies: For each challenge listed above, write down one strategy that could help mitigate that challenge.

2. Creating a Support System

Identify the key people in your support system and describe how they can assist in managing ADHD.

A. Support Person 1 : _____

B. Support Person 2 : _____

C. Support Person 3: _____

7.3 Putting Theory into Practice

Exercise 1: Role-Playing a Challenging Scenario

With a partner, act out a challenging situation related to ADHD. Swap roles to gain different perspectives. Reflect on what strategies worked and what could be improved.

Exercise 2: Creating a Weekly Schedule

Develop a weekly schedule that incorporates the strategies learned in this book. Include specific goals, supportive environments, and breaks for leisure and relaxation.

Example

Day	Time	Activity/ Task	Specific Goal	Supportive Environment	Leisure/ Relaxation
Monday	7-8 AM	Morning Routine	Get ready for the day	Calm, structured home	Breakfast together
	9 AM-12 PM	School/ Work	Focus on key tasks	Supportive classroom/ Office	Short breaks
	1-3 PM	Homework/ Project Work	Complete assignments	Quiet study room	Snack time
	4-5 PM	Exercise/ Outdoor Play	Physical activity	Park or gym	Fun playtime
	6-8 PM	Family Dinner & Relax	Bonding time	Warm family setting	Movie time
Tuesday	...	...	...	...	...
Wednesday	...	...	...	...	...
Thursday	...	...	...	...	...
Friday	...	...	...	...	...
Saturday	...	...	...	...	...
Sunday	...	...	...	...	...

Exercise 3: ADHD Behavior Tracker

This worksheet helps in monitoring and understanding specific ADHD behaviors. By tracking the frequency, triggers, and responses, parents and teachers can gain insights into what might be causing or exacerbating symptoms.

- **Date and Time:** Record when the behavior occurred.
- **Behavior Observed:** Describe the specific behavior (e.g., inattention, impulsivity).
- **Possible Triggers:** Note any potential triggers or contributing factors.
- **Response and Outcome:** Detail how you responded and the outcome.

Exercise 4: Homework and Study Planner

Help your ADHD-affected child stay on track with homework and studying using this planner.

- **Subject:** List the subjects for study or homework.
- **Tasks:** Break down each subject into manageable tasks.
- **Time Required:** Estimate the time required for each task.
- **Breaks and Rewards:** Plan breaks and rewards to maintain motivation.

Exercise 5: Daily Routine Chart

A consistent daily routine can support children with ADHD. Use this chart to create a predictable pattern for your child.

- **Morning Routine:** Outline the morning steps, from waking up to leaving for school.
- **After School Routine:** Plan activities, homework, and relaxation time.
- **Evening Routine:** Include dinner, family time, and bedtime preparation.

Exercise 6: Positive Reinforcement Log

Positive reinforcement can be a powerful tool. Track what rewards and positive reinforcements are working.

- **Behavior Goal:** Define the specific behavior you want to encourage.
- **Reward:** Decide on an appropriate reward for achieving the goal.
- **Achievement Date:** Record when the child successfully reached the goal.

Exercise 7: Family Communication Planner

Enhance communication within the family, especially around ADHD-related challenges.

- **Family Meeting Time:** Schedule regular family meetings.
- **Discussion Topics:** List topics to discuss, including successes and areas for improvement.
- **Action Steps:** Outline agreed-upon actions and responsibilities.

8 THANKS

In this book, I have included all the knowledge, strategies, and solutions I have learned in 20 years of work and continuous study. I hope you have enjoyed this publication, which took me months of work and sacrifice. Thank you for purchasing my book. I have a GIFT FOR YOU: a free video course regarding "How to Discipline Your Child with ADHD."
You can download this bonus for free from this link:

https://dl.bookfunnel.com/b8yw5x4m7t

Thank you for reading this book; it was not easy to make this publication. I hope it will be useful to you, and I would be happy to receive your opinion with an unbiased and honest review; it would mean a lot to me and help me improve in future publications.

Thank you very much. I hope to update the book soon with lots of new tips. I will look forward to your best suggestions.

Jennifer Mindlin

Made in United States
Troutdale, OR
09/26/2023

13200140R00066